THE COOK'S ENCYCLOPEDIA OF

BEST-EVER PASTA COOKING

THE COOK'S ENCYCLOPEDIA OF

BEST-EVER PASTA COOKING

CONSULTANT EDITOR: LINDA FRASER

This edition is published by Hermes House

Hermes House is an imprint of Anness Publishing Ltd
Hermes House, 88–89 Blackfriars Road, London SE1 8HA
tel. 020 7401 2077; fax 020 7633 9499; info@anness.com

A CIP catalogue record for this book is available from the British Library.

Publisher: Joanna Lorenz
Senior Cookery Editor: Linda Fraser
Cookery Editor: Ann Hildyard
Copy Editor: Val Barrett
Designer: Bill Mason
Photography and styling: Patrick McLeavey, assisted by Jo Brewer
Food for Photography: Jane Stevenson assisted by Lucy McElvie
Illustrator: Madeleine David

Previously published as *Best Ever Pasta*

1 3 5 7 9 10 8 6 4 2

NOTES

For all recipes, quantities are given in both metric and imperial measures and, where appropriate, measures are also given in standard cups and spoons.
Follow one set, but not a mixture because they are not interchangeable.

Standard spoon and cup measurements are level.
1 tbsp = 15ml, 1 tsp = 5ml, 1 cup = 250ml/8fl oz

Australian standard tablespoons are 20ml. Australian readers should use 3 tsp in place of 1 tbsp for measuring small quantities of gelatine, cornflour, salt etc.
Size 3 (medium) eggs should be used unless otherwise stated.

Contents

Introduction 6

Equipment 12

Soups with Pasta 20

Pasta with Fish & Seafood 36

Meals in Minutes 72

Salads & Starters 108

Midweek Meals 130

Quick & Easy 166

Simple Suppers 202

Pasta Sauces 238

Index 254

Introduction

PASTA HAS RAPIDLY become one of Western society's staple foods, travelling across the world in various forms from Asia and South America. Its origins are unclear, but a type of pasta was certainly made in Sicily, the "grain store" of Rome, in the days of the Roman Empire. It has also existed in China and Japan for many centuries, but in very different forms and shapes.

The enormous popularity of pasta is due to its incredible versatility, and its value for money. Pasta can stretch a few store-cupboard ingredients to make a satisfying meal fit for a king! You can produce sauces with small amounts of meat, mix them with pasta and produce a filling and nutritious dish. Most wheat-flour-and-water (commercial dried) pasta contains more proteins and carbohydrates than potatoes, so when combined with a sauce of vegetables, cheese or meat, it gives a good nutritional balance. It is a fine source of energy too – better than sugar, as it releases energy at a slower prolonged rate, and will give you a lift if you are tired and hungry. Pasta is only fattening if eaten in over-large quantities with too much sauce! Italians fill up on the pasta itself, the sauce being an adornment to enhance the flavour.

Pasta is very easy to make at home if you have patience and a little time to spare. The result is exciting and delicious, even if it is a little soggy to begin with! It's a little like making bread: once you have mastered the technique, you can make one of life's staples.

The recipes in this book are mostly based on a family of four people, but they can be easily halved for two or doubled for eight. There are chapters on soups, fish and seafood, salads and starters and sauces, as well as suggestions, meals in minutes, midweek meals, quick and easy dishes and simple suppers to provide you with a best-ever pasta meal for every occasion.

Pasta Types

When buying dried pasta, choose good-quality well-known brands. Of the "fresh" pasta sold in sealed packs in supermarkets, the filled or stuffed varieties are worth buying; noodles and ribbon pasta are better bought dried, as these tend to have more bite when cooked. However, if you are lucky enough to live near an Italian delicatessen where pasta is made on the premises, it will usually be of very good quality. Fresh is not necessarily better, but the final choice is yours – the best pasta is home-made, as then you can be sure of the quality of the ingredients used and also of the finished texture.

You will see from this book that the sauces are almost limitless in their variety, as are the pasta shapes themselves. There are no hard-and-fast rules regarding which shape to use with which pasta sauce: it's really a matter of personal preference. However, there are a few guidelines to follow, such as that thin spaghetti suits seafood sauces, thicker spaghetti is good with creamy sauces (as in, for instance, Spaghetti alla Carbonara) and thick tubular pasta, like rigatoni, penne and so on, suits rustic sauces full of bits that will be caught in the pasta itself.

fresh pappardelle
wholemeal spaghetti
tomato spaghetti
spinach spaghetti
fresh beetroot tagliatelle
pipe rigate
fresh wild-mushroom tagliatelle
campanelle
conchigliette
farfalle (pasta bows)
fettuccia riccia
ne lunghe
cannelloni
spirali
rigatoni
pasta shells (conchiglie)
lasagne
spinach lasagne
orecchiette
garganelle
wholemeal shells

Sauces and Pastes

There is an infinite variety of ready-made sauces and pastes available which you can add to your own sauce to make it richer or to deepen the flavour. Some can even be incorporated into pasta dough: for example, you can make mushroom or tomato or even pesto pasta.

Anchovies: salted Whole anchovies preserved in salt need to be rinsed and the backbone removed before use. They have a fresher flavour than canned anchovy fillets in oil. Used in moderation, anchovies add a fishy depth to sauces and soups.

Capers These are little green flower buds preserved in vinegar or salt. They add a sharp piquancy to rich sauces and are particularly good with tomatoes and many cheeses.

Carbonara sauce Although your own version made from the recipe in this book will be much better, ready-made carbonara sauce is a useful standby for a quick meal – add sautéed fresh mushrooms or more bacon to make it go further.

Garlic: chopped A great time-saver, eliminating the need for peeling and chopping. Use it straight out of the jar.

Mushroom paste A delicacy available from Italian delicatessens. Add a generous spoonful to freshly cooked pasta with a little cream for a quick sauce, or incorporate into dough to make delicious mushroom pasta.

Olive paste Cuts out all that stoning and chopping. Delicious stirred into hot pasta with chopped fresh tomato or added by the spoonful to enrich a tomato or meat sauce.

Pesto The commercial version of fresh basil pesto. Brands vary, but it is a very useful store-cupboard standby to stir into hot pasta and soups.

Pesto: fresh Some supermarkets produce their own "fresh" pesto, sold in tubs in the chilled cabinet. This is infinitely superior to the bottled variety, although your own freshly made pesto will be even better.

Pesto: red A commercial sauce made from tomatoes and red peppers to stir into hot pasta or to pep up soups.

Tomato pasta sauce Again, a good standby or base for a quick meal. Vary by adding chopped anchovies and olives, or pour over freshly cooked stuffed pasta such as tortellini.

Tomato purée An essential if you are making a sauce from insipid fresh tomatoes. It will intensify any tomato-based sauce and will help thicken meat sauces. It will also make tomato pasta if added to the basic dough ingredients.

Tomatoes: canned plum No store-cupboard should be without these – invaluable for making any tomato sauce or stew when good fresh tomatoes are not readily available.

Tomatoes: canned chopped Usually made from Italian plum tomatoes which have a fuller flavour than most, these are the heart of a good tomato sauce if you cannot find really ripe, red, tasty, fresh tomatoes.

Tomatoes: passata A useful store-cupboard ingredient, this is pulped tomato that has been strained to remove the seeds. It makes a good base for a tomato sauce, though chopped canned tomatoes can also be used.

Tomatoes: sun-dried in oil These tomatoes are drained and chopped and added to tomato-based dishes to give a deeper, almost roasted tomato flavour.

Below, clockwise from top left: Salted anchovies; canned chopped tomatoes; pesto; olive paste; canned plum tomatoes; tomato purée; passata.

Eastern Pasta

Various forms of noodle or pasta exist outside Europe and America. They are found mainly in China and Japan, but also throughout Malaysia, Hong Kong and the rest of the Far East, including parts of India and Tibet.

This pasta, usually in noodle form and often enhanced with a sprinkling of vegetables or fish, adds variety to the sometimes monotonous staple diet of rice and beans eaten by the poorer sections of the population. Some types of pasta are used to give bulk to soups; others are eaten as a filling dish to stave off hunger during the day. They are made from the staple crops of each region – whether rice flour, soya bean flour or potato flour – and are cooked in different ways: some are soaked and then fried, some are boiled and fried and some are rolled out and stuffed like ravioli, but most are simply boiled. Some turn transparent when cooked.

Oriental egg noodles are usually made with wheat flour and can be treated in the same way as ordinary Western pasta. Buckwheat and fresh wholemeal noodles are cooked in a similar fashion. Fresh white noodles do not contain egg but are cooked in the same way as egg noodles. Some dried egg noodles come in discs or blocks and are "cooked" by immersion in boiling water in which they are then left to soak for a few minutes. As with Western pasta, oriental noodles can be flavoured with additional ingredients such as prawns, carrot and spinach.

Won ton skins, like thin squares of rolled-out pasta, are used for stuffing and making different filled shapes. Although oriental pasta is available in a variety of long noodle types, it doesn't seem to be made into the shapes we are used to seeing in Europe and America: you will often find it wound into balls and beautifully packaged.

Above: Eastern noodles include (from top left, clockwise) oriental rice flour noodles, rice vermicelli, rice stick noodles, handmade amoy flour vermicelli, medium egg noodles, fresh brown mein, egg noodles, rice stick vermicelli, fresh thin egg noodles, Japanese wheat flour noodles, Ho Fan vermicelli, spinach vegetable noodles, carrot vegetable noodles, won ton skins, wheat flour noodles, fresh white mein, buckwheat noodles, shrimp egg noodles.

Equipment

To make pasta, a bare minimum of equipment is needed – practised hands would say that only a clean work surface and a rolling pin were strictly necessary. However, there are several gadgets to assist the pasta maker.

Bowls A set of bowls is useful for mixing, whisking and so on.
Chopping board A hygienic nylon board is recommended for cutting and chopping.
Colander A large colander is essential for draining cooked pasta quickly.
Cook's knife A large all-purpose cook's knife is necesary for cutting pasta and for chopping.
Flour dredger This is useful for dusting pasta with small amounts of flour.
Large metal spoon For folding in and serving sauces.
Measuring spoons For accurately measuring small quantities of ingredients for pasta.
Pasta machine or roller Vital for kneading, rolling and cutting pasta – a real labour-saver. Attachments for other shapes are available.
Pasta or pastry wheel For cutting pasta with a decorated edge, such as pasta bows.
Pastry brush For removing excess flour from pasta and for brushing pasta with water, milk or beaten egg to seal.
Pestle and mortar For hand-grinding pesto and crushing black peppercorns.
Ravioli cutter For cutting or stamping out individual raviolis; can be round or square. A selection of pastry cutters will serve the same purpose.
Ravioli tray (raviolatore) For making sheets of ravioli quickly and neatly – with practice.
Rolling pin Pasta pins are available in specialist shops. These are long, thin and tapered at each end, but you have to be quite adept to use them. An ordinary heavy wooden rolling pin will do instead.
Slotted spoon Useful for draining small amounts of food.
Small grater For grating nutmeg and Parmesan cheese
Vegetable knife For preparing vegetables and paring lemons, and for delicate work.
Vegetable peeler For shaving Parmesan cheese, and chocolate for sweet pasta.
Whisk Essential for beating eggs thoroughly and combining sauces smoothly.

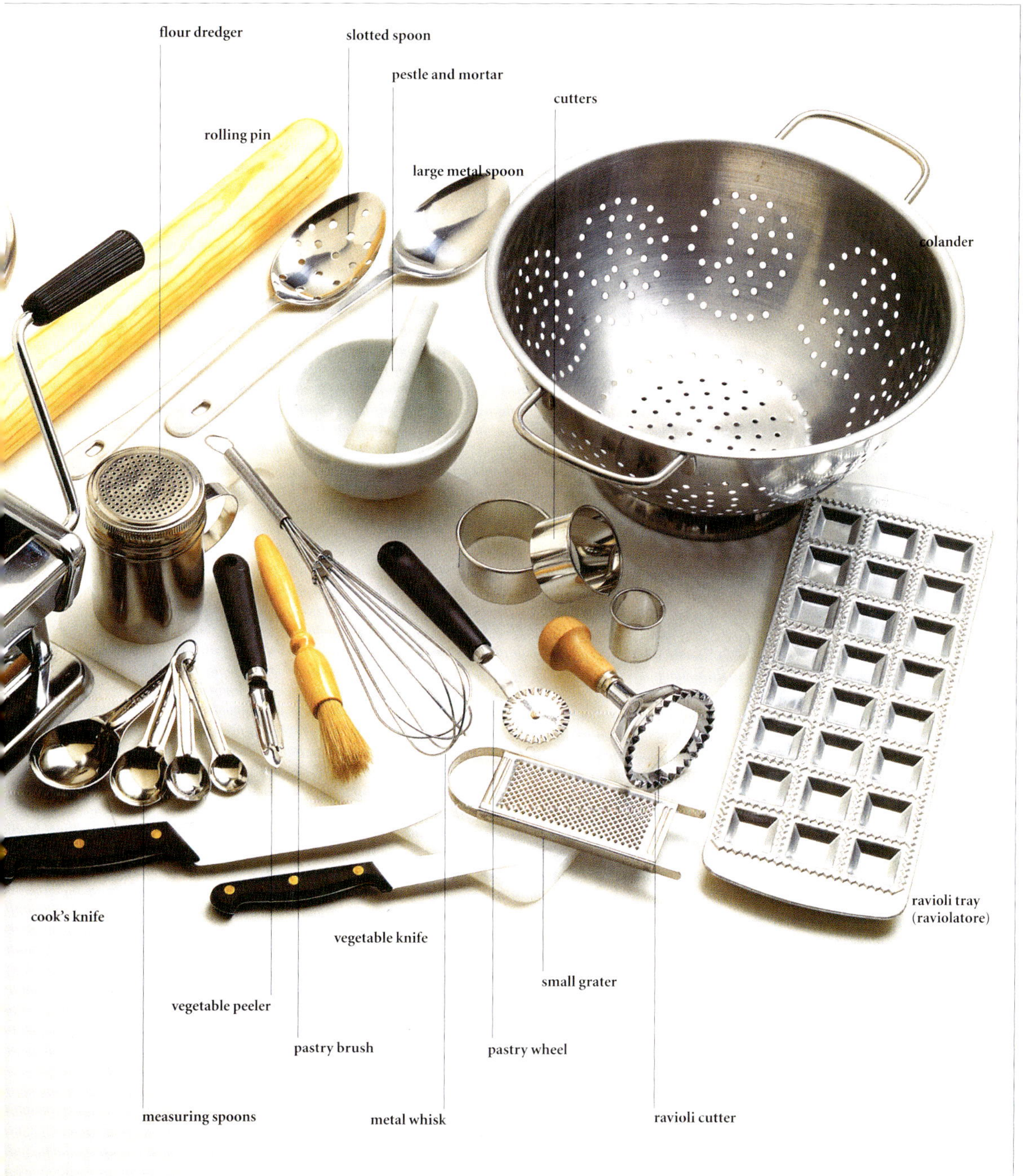
flour dredger
slotted spoon
pestle and mortar
cutters
rolling pin
large metal spoon
colander
ravioli tray
(raviolatore)
cook's knife
vegetable knife
small grater
vegetable peeler
pastry brush
pastry wheel
measuring spoons
metal whisk
ravioli cutter

About Pasta

Most pasta is made from durum wheat flour and water – durum is a special kind of wheat with a very high protein content. Egg pasta, *pasta all'uova*, contains flour and eggs, and is used for flat pasta such as tagliatelle, or for lasagne. Very little wholemeal pasta is eaten in Italy, but it is quite popular in other countries.

All these types of pasta are available dried in packets and will keep almost indefinitely. Fresh pasta is now widely available and can be bought in most good supermarkets. It can be very good, but can never compare to home-made egg pasta.

Pasta comes in countless shapes and sizes. It is very difficult to give a definitive list, as the names for the shapes vary from country to country. In some cases, just within Italy, the same shape can appear with several different names, depending upon which region it is in. The pasta shapes called for in this book, as well as many others, are illustrated in the introduction. The most common names have been listed there.

Most of the recipes in this book specify the pasta shape most appropriate for a particular sauce. They can, of course, be replaced with another kind. A general rule is that long pasta goes better with tomato or thinner sauces, while short pasta is best for chunkier, meatier sauces. But this rule should not be followed too rigidly. Part of the fun of cooking and eating pasta is in the endless possible combinations of sauce and pasta shapes.

How to Make Egg Pasta by Hand

This classic recipe for egg pasta from Emilia Romagna region, around Bolognia, calls for just three ingredients; flour, eggs and a little salt. In other regions of Italy water, milk or oil are sometimes added. Use plain or strong white flour, and large eggs. As a general guide, use 50g/2oz/½ cup of flour to each egg. Quantities will vary with the exact size of the eggs.

To serve 3–4
150g/5oz/1¼ cups flour
2 eggs
pinch of salt

To serve 4–6
210g/7½oz/scant 2 cups flour
3 eggs
pinch of salt

To serve 6–8
275g/10oz/2½ cups flour
4 eggs
pinch of salt

1 Place the flour in the centre of a clean, smooth work surface. Make a well in the middle. Break the eggs into the well. Add a pinch of salt.

2 Start beating the eggs with a fork, gradually drawing the flour from the inside walls of the well. As the pasta thickens, continue the mixing with your hands. Incorporate as much flour as possible until the mixture forms a mass. It will still be lumpy. If it still sticks to your hands, add a little more flour. Set the dough aside. Scrape off all traces of the dough from the work surface until it is perfectly smooth. Wash and dry your hands.

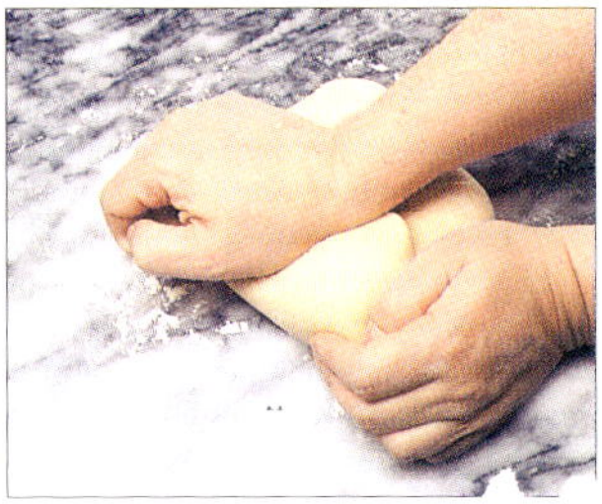

3 Lightly flour the work surface. Knead the dough by pressing it away from you with the heel of your hands, and then folding it over towards you. Repeat this action over and over, turning the dough as you knead. Work for about 10 minutes, or until the dough is smooth and elastic.

4 If you are using more than two eggs, divide the dough in half. Flour the rolling pin and the work surface. Pat the dough into a disc and begin rolling it out into a flat circle, rotating it a quarter turn after each roll to keep its shape round. Roll until the disc is about 3mm/⅛in thick.

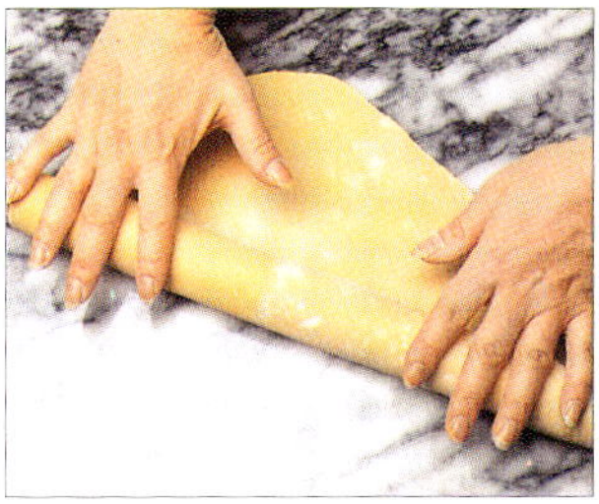

5 Roll out the dough until it is paper-thin by rolling up on to the rolling pin and simultaneously giving a sideways stretch with your hands. Wrap the near edge of the dough around the centre of the rolling pin and begin rolling the dough up away from you. As you roll back and forth, slide your hands from the centre towards the outer edges of the pin, stretching and thinning out the pasta.

6 Quickly repeat these movements until about two-thirds of the sheet of pasta is wrapped around the pin. Lift and turn the wrapped pasta sheet about 45° before unrolling it. Repeat the rolling and stretch process, starting from a new point of the sheet each

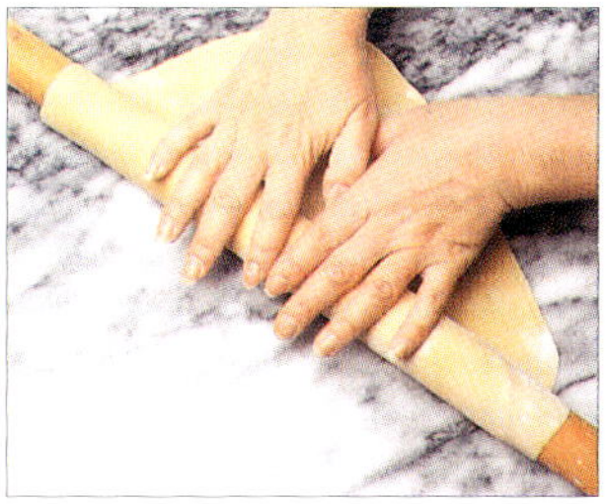

time to keep it evenly thin. By the end (this process should not last more than 8 to 10 minutes or the dough will lose its elasticity) the whole sheet should be smooth and almost transparent. If the dough is still sticky, lightly flour your hands as you continue rolling and stretching it in the same way.

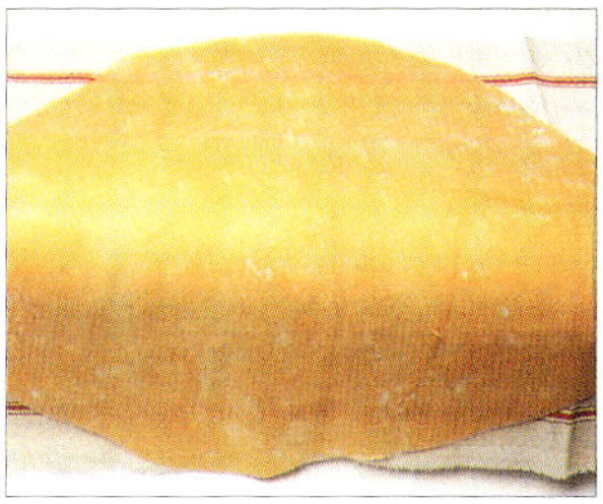

7 If you are making pasta noodles, such as tagliatelle, fettuccine, etc, lay a clean dish towel on a table or other flat surface, and unroll the pasta sheet onto it, letting about one-third of the sheet hang over the edge of the table. Rotate the dough about every 10 minutes. Roll out the second sheet of dough if you are using more than two eggs. After 25–30 minutes the pasta will have dried enough to cut. Do not allow to overdry or the pasta will crack as it is cut.

8 To cut tagliatelle, fettuccine or tagliolini, fold the sheet of pasta into a flat roll about 10cm/4in wide. Cut across the roll to form noodles of the desired width. Tagliolini is 3mm/⅛in; fettuccine is 4mm/⅙in; tagliatelle is 5mm/¼in. After cutting, open out the noodles and let them dry for about 5 minutes before cooking. These noodles may be stored for some weeks without refrigeration. Allow the noodles to dry completely before storing them, uncovered, in a dry cupboard, and use as required.

9 To cut the pasta for lasagne or pappardelle, do not fold or dry the rolled-out dough. Lasagne is made from rectangles approximately 13 × 9cm/5 × 3½in. Pappardelle are large noodles cut with a fluted pasta or pastry wheel. They are about 2cm/¾in wide.

Egg Pasta Made by Machine

Making pasta with a machine is quick and easy. The results are perhaps not quite as fine as with handmade pasta, but they are certainly better than ready-made pastas will ever be.

You will need a pasta-making machine, either hand-cranked or electric. Use the same proportions of eggs, flour and salt as for Handmade Egg Pasta.

1 Place the flour in the centre of a clean smooth work surface. Make a well in the middle. Break the eggs into the well. Add a pinch of salt. Start beating the eggs with a fork, gradually drawing the flour from the inside walls of the well. As the paste thickens, continue mixing with your hands. Incorporate as much flour as possible until the mixture forms a mass. It will still be lumpy. If it sticks to your hands, add a little more flour. Set the dough aside and scrape the work surface clean.

2 Set the machine rollers at their widest (kneading) setting. Pull off a piece of dough the size of a small orange. Place the remaining dough between two soup plates. Feed the dough through the rollers. Fold it in half, end to end, and feed it through again about 7–8 times, turning it and folding it over after each kneading. The dough should be smooth and fairly evenly rectangular. If it sticks to the machine, brush with flour. Lay it out on a lightly floured work surface or on a clean dish towel, and repeat with the remaining dough, broken into pieces roughly the same size.

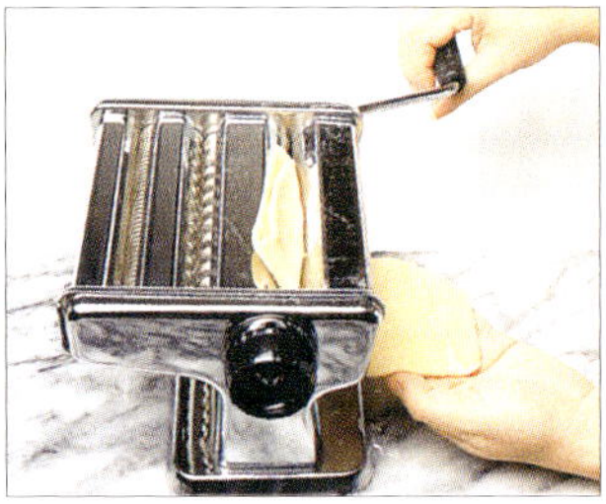

3 Adjust the machine to the next line setting. Feed each strip through once only, and replace on the drying surface. Keep them in the order in which they were first kneaded.

4 Reset the machine to the next setting. Repeat, passing each strip through once. Repeat for each remaining roller setting until the pasta is the right thickness – for most purposes this is given by the next to last setting, except for very delicate strips such as tagliolini, or for ravioli. If the pasta strips get too long, cut them in half to allow for easier handling.

5 Be sure the pasta is fairly dry, but not brittle, or the noodles may stick together when cut. Select the desired width of cutter, and feed the strips through.

6 Separate the noodles, and leave to dry for at least 15 minutes before using. They may be stored for some weeks without refrigeration. Allow them to dry completely before storing them, uncovered, in a dry cupboard. They may also be frozen, first loose on trays and then packed together.

7 If you are making stuffed pasta, such as ravioli, cannelloni, etc, do not let the pasta strips dry out before filling them, but proceed immediately with the individual recipe of your choice.

GREEN PASTA

Follow the same recipe, adding 50g/2oz/¼ cup cooked, very finely chopped, spinach (which has been squeezed very dry) to the eggs and flour. You may have to add a little more flour to absorb the moisture from the spinach. This pasta is very suitable for stuffed recipes, as it seals better than plain egg pasta.

How to Cook Dried Pasta

Ready-made and homemade pasta are cooked in the same way, though the timings vary greatly. Home-made pasta cooks virtually in the time it takes for the water to return to the boil after it is put in the pan.

1 Always cook pasta in a large amount of rapidly boiling water. Use at least 1–2 litres/ $1^3/_4$-$3^1/_2$ pints/4-8 cups water to each 115g/4oz pasta.

2 The water should be salted at least 2 minutes before the pasta is added, to give the salt time to dissolve. Add 25ml/$1^1/_2$ tbsp salt per 450g/1lb pasta. You may want to vary the saltiness of the cooking water.

3 Drop the pasta into the boiling water all at once. Use a wooden spoon to help ease long pasta in as it softens, to prevent it from breaking. Stir frequently to prevent the pasta sticking together or to the pan. Cook the pasta at a fast boil, but be prepared to lower the heat if it boils over.

4 Timing is critical in pasta cooking. Follow the instructions on the packet for ready-made pasta, but it is best in all cases to test for readiness by tasting. In Italy pasta is always eaten *al dente*, which means firm to the bite. Cooked this way it is just tender, but its "soul" (the innermost part) is still firm. Overcooked pasta will be mushy.

5 Place a colander in the sink before the pasta has finished cooking. As soon as the pasta is done, tip it all into the colander (you may first want to reserve a cupful of the hot cooking water to add to the sauce if it needs thinning). Shake the colander lightly to remove most but not all of the cooking water. Pasta should never be over-drained.

6 Quickly turn the pasta into a warmed serving dish and immediately toss it with a little butter or oil, or the prepared sauce. Alternatively, turn it into the cooking pan with the sauce, where it will be cooked for a further 1–2 minutes as it is mixed into the sauce. Never allow pasta to sit undressed, as it will stick together and become unpalatable.

How to Cook Egg Pasta

Fresh egg pasta, especially home-made, cooks very much faster than dried pasta. Make sure everything is ready (the sauce and serving dishes) before you start boiling egg pasta, as there will not be time once the cooking starts, and egg pasta becomes soft and mushy very quickly if left too long.

1 Always cook pasta in a large amount of rapidly boiling water. Use at least 1–2 litres/ $1^3/_4$-$3^1/_2$ pints/4-8 cups water to a quantity of pasta made with 115g/4oz/1 cup flour. Salt the water as you would for dried pasta.

2 Drop the pasta into the boiling water all at once. Stir gently to prevent the pasta sticking together or to the pan. Cook the pasta at a fast boil.

3 Freshly made pasta can be done as little as 15 seconds after the cooking water comes back to the boil. Stuffed pasta takes a few minutes longer. When done, tip the pasta into the colander and proceed as for dried pasta.

Macaroni

Macaroni is the generic name for any hollow pasta. This method is for making garganelle.

1 Cut squares of pasta dough using a sharp knife on a floured surface.

2 Wrap the squares around a pencil or chopstick on the diagonal to form tubes. Slip off and allow to dry slightly.

SPINACH PASTA

Use 150g/5oz frozen leaf spinach, cooked and squeezed dry, a pinch of salt, 2 eggs, about 200g/7oz/1¾ cups plain white flour, or a little more if the pasta is sticky. Proceed as for Basic Pasta Dough, but liquidize the spinach with the eggs to give a fine texture.

Tagliatelle

Tagliatelle can also be made with a pasta machine, but it is fairly straightforward to make by hand.

1 Roll up the floured pasta dough like a Swiss roll.

2 Cut the roll into thin slices with a very sharp knife. Immediately unravel the slices to reveal the pasta ribbons. To make taglianni, cut the slices about 3mm/⅛in thick.

3 To make pappardelle, using a serrated pastry wheel, cut out wide ribbons from the rolled-out pastry dough.

Tortellini

Tortellini or "little twists" can be made with meat or vegetarian fillings and served with sauce or in a hearty soup.

1 Using a round biscuit cutter, stamp out rounds of pasta.

2 Pipe or spoon the chosen filling into the middle of each of the rounds.

3 Brush the edges with beaten egg and fold the round into a crescent shape, excluding all the air. Bend the two corners round to meet each other and press well to seal. Repeat with the remaining dough. Leave to dry on a floured dish towel for 30 minutes before cooking the tortellini.

SPINACH, RICOTTA AND PARMESAN FILLING FOR STUFFED PASTA

Serves 4–6

450g/1lb frozen spinach, thawed and squeezed dry
2.5ml/½ tsp grated nutmeg
5ml/1 tsp salt
ground black pepper
175g/6oz/¾ cup fresh ricotta or curd cheese
25g/1oz/¼ cup freshly grated Parmesan cheese

Place all the ingredients in a blender or food processor and process until smooth. Use as required in your recipe.

Ravioli

Although ravioli can be bought ready made, the very best is made at home. Serve with sauce or in a soup.

1 Cut the dough in half and wrap one portion in clear film. Roll out the pasta thinly to a rectangle on a lightly floured surface. Cover with a clean, damp dish towel and repeat with the remaining pasta. Pipe small mounds (about 5ml/1 tsp) of filling in even rows, spacing them at 4cm/1½in intervals, across one piece of the dough. Brush the spaces between the filling with egg.

2 Using a rolling pin, lift the second sheet of pasta over the dough with the filling. Press down firmly between the pockets of filling, pushing out any air.

3 Cut into squares with a serrated ravioli cutter or sharp knife. Transfer to a floured dish towel and rest for 1 hour before cooking the ravioli.

Soups with Pasta

Pasta, Bean and Vegetable Soup

This colourful, filling soup will satisfy the largest appetite.

INGREDIENTS

Serves 4–6

115g/4oz dried borlotti or black-eyed beans, soaked overnight and drained
1.2 litres/2 pints/5 cups vegetable, poultry or meat stock
1 large onion, chopped
1 large garlic clove, finely chopped
2 celery sticks, chopped
½ red pepper, seeded and chopped
350g/12oz tomatoes, skinned, seeded and chopped or canned chopped tomatoes
225g/8oz smoked bacon loin
75g/3oz tiny soup pasta
2 courgettes, halved lengthways and sliced
15ml/1 tbsp tomato purée
salt and ground black pepper
shredded fresh basil, to garnish

1 Put the beans in a large pan. Cover with fresh cold water and bring to the boil. Boil for 10 minutes, then drain and rinse. Return the beans to the pan, add the stock and bring to the boil. Skim off the scum.

2 Add the onion, garlic, celery, red pepper, tomatoes and bacon. Bring back to the boil.

3 Cover and simmer over a low heat for 1½ hours or until the beans are just tender. Lift out the bacon. Shred the meat coarsely with two forks and set aside.

4 Add the pasta, courgettes and tomato purée to the soup. Season to taste with salt and pepper. Simmer uncovered, for a further 5–8 minutes, stirring the soup occasionally. (Check the pasta cooking time on the packet.)

5 Stir in the shredded bacon. Taste and adjust the seasoning if necessary, then serve the soup hot, sprinkled with shredded fresh basil as a garnish.

Chunky Pasta Soup

Serve this filling main-meal soup with tasty, pesto-topped French bread croûtons.

INGREDIENTS

Serves 4

115g/4oz/⅔ cup dry beans (a mixture of red kidney and haricot beans), soaked in cold water overnight
15ml/1 tbsp oil
1 onion, chopped
2 celery sticks, thinly sliced
2–3 garlic cloves, crushed
2 leeks, thinly sliced
1 vegetable stock cube
400g/14oz can or jar of pimientos
45–60ml/3–4 tbsp tomato purée
115g/4oz pasta shapes
4 pieces French bread
15ml/1 tbsp pesto sauce
115g/4oz/1 cup baby sweetcorn, halved
50g/2oz each broccoli and cauliflower florets
few drops of Tabasco sauce, to taste
salt and ground black pepper

1 Drain the beans and place in a large saucepan with 1.2 litres/2 pints/5 cups water. Bring to the boil and simmer for about 1 hour, or until nearly tender.

2 When the beans are almost ready, heat the oil in a large pan and fry the vegetables for 2 minutes. Add the stock cube and the beans with 600ml/1 pint/2 cups of their liquid. Cover and simmer for 10 minutes.

3 Meanwhile, purée the pimientos with a little of their liquid and add to the pan. Stir in the tomato purée and pasta and cook for 15 minutes. Preheat the oven to 200°C/400°F/Gas 6.

4 Meanwhile, make the pesto croûtons; spread the French bread with the pesto sauce and bake for 10 minutes, or until crispy.

5 When the pasta is just cooked, add the sweetcorn, broccoli and cauliflower florets, Tabasco sauce and seasoning to taste. Heat through for 2–3 minutes and serve at once with the croûtons.

Thai Chicken Soup

This classic Oriental soup now enjoys worldwide popularity.

INGREDIENTS

Serves 4

15ml/1 tbsp vegetable oil
1 garlic clove, finely chopped
2 boneless chicken breasts, about 175g/6oz each, skinned and chopped
2.5ml/½ tsp ground turmeric
1.5ml/¼ tsp hot chilli powder
75g/3oz creamed coconut
900ml/1½ pints/3¾ cups hot chicken stock
30ml/2 tbsp lemon or lime juice
30ml/2 tbsp crunchy peanut butter
50g/2oz thread egg noodles, broken into small pieces
15ml/1 tbsp spring onions, finely chopped
15ml/1 tbsp chopped fresh coriander
salt and ground black pepper
30ml/2 tbsp desiccated coconut and ½ fresh red chilli, seeded and finely chopped, to garnish

1 Heat the oil in a large pan and fry the garlic for 1 minute until lightly golden. Add the chicken and spices and stir-fry for a further 3–4 minutes.

2 Crumble the creamed coconut into the hot chicken stock and stir until dissolved. Pour on to the chicken then add the lemon or lime juice, peanut butter and egg noodles.

3 Cover and simmer for about 15 minutes. Add the spring onions and fresh coriander, then season well and cook for a further 5 minutes.

4 Meanwhile, place the desiccated coconut and chilli in a small frying pan and heat for 2–3 minutes, stirring frequently, until the coconut is lightly browned.

5 Serve the soup in warmed bowls sprinkled with the fried coconut and chilli.

Classic Minestrone

This famous Italian soup has been much imitated around the world – with varying results. The home-made version is a delicious revelation and mouthwateringly healthy with pasta, beans and lots of fresh vegetables.

INGREDIENTS

Serves 4

1 large leek, thinly sliced
2 carrots, chopped
1 courgette, thinly sliced
115g/4oz whole green beans, halved
2 celery sticks, thinly sliced
45ml/3 tbsp olive oil
1.5 litres/2½ pints/6¼ cups stock or water
400g/14oz can chopped tomatoes
15ml/1 tbsp chopped fresh basil
5ml/1 tsp chopped fresh thyme or 2.5ml/½ tsp dried
salt and ground black pepper
400g/14oz can cannellini or kidney beans
50g/2oz small pasta shapes or macaroni
finely grated Parmesan cheese, to garnish (optional)
fresh parsley, chopped, to garnish

1 Put all the fresh vegetables into a large saucepan with the olive oil. Heat until sizzling then cover, lower the heat and sweat the vegetables for 15 minutes, shaking the pan occasionally.

2 Add the stock or water, tomatoes, herbs and seasoning. Bring to the boil, replace the lid and simmer gently for about 30 minutes.

3 Add the canned beans and their liquor together with the pasta, and simmer for a further 10 minutes. Check the seasoning and serve hot, sprinkled with the Parmesan cheese, if using, and chopped fresh parsley.

COOK'S TIP

Minestrone is also delicious served cold on a hot summer's day. In fact the flavour improves if made a day or two ahead and stored in the fridge. It can also be frozen and reheated.

Pea and Ham Soup

Frozen peas provide flavour, freshness and colour in this delicious winter soup, which is filling enough to make a light main course or can be served as a starter.

INGREDIENTS

Serves 4

115g/4oz small pasta shapes
30ml/2 tbsp vegetable oil
1 small bunch spring onions, chopped
350g/12oz/3 cups frozen peas
1.2 litres/2 pints/5 cups chicken stock
225g/8oz raw unsmoked ham or gammon
60ml/4 tbsp double cream
salt and ground black pepper
warm crusty bread, to serve

1 Cook the small pasta shapes in plenty of boiling salted water according to the packet instructions. Drain through a colander, place in the pan again, cover with cold water and set aside until required.

2 Heat the vegetable oil in a large heavy saucepan and cook the spring onions gently until soft but not browned. Add the frozen peas and chicken stock, then simmer gently over a low heat for about 10 minutes.

3 Process the soup in a blender or food processor then return to the saucepan. Cut the ham or gammon into short fingers and add, with the pasta, to the saucepan. Simmer for 2–3 minutes and season to taste. Stir in the double cream and serve immediately with the warm crusty bread.

Consommé with Agnolotti

A delicious and satisfying consommé with wonderful flavours.

INGREDIENTS

Serves 4–6

75g/3oz cooked peeled prawns
75g/3oz canned crab meat, drained
5ml/1 tsp fresh root ginger, peeled and finely grated
15ml/1 tbsp fresh white breadcrumbs
5ml/1 tsp light soy sauce
1 spring onion, finely chopped
1 garlic clove, crushed
1 quantity of basic pasta dough
flour, for dusting
egg white, beaten
400g/14oz can chicken or fish consommé
30ml/2 tbsp sherry or vermouth
salt and ground black pepper
50g/2oz cooked, peeled prawns and fresh coriander leaves, to garnish

1 To make the filling, put the prawns, crab meat, ginger, breadcrumbs, soy sauce, onion, garlic and seasoning into a food processor or blender and process until smooth.

2 Roll the pasta into thin sheets and dust lightly with flour. Stamp out 32 rounds 5cm/2in in diameter, with a fluted pastry cutter.

3 Place a small teaspoon of the filling in the centre of half the pasta rounds. Brush the edges of each round with egg white and sandwich together with a second round on top. Pinch the edges together firmly to stop the filling seeping out.

4 Cook the pasta in a large pan of boiling salted water for 5 minutes (cook in batches to stop them sticking together). Remove and drop into a bowl of cold water for 5 seconds before placing on a tray. (You can make these pasta shapes a day in advance. Cover with clear film and store in the fridge until required.)

5 Heat the chicken or fish consommé in a pan with the sherry or vermouth. When piping hot, add the pasta shapes and simmer for 1–2 minutes.

6 Serve in a shallow soup bowl covered with hot consommé. Garnish with extra peeled prawns and fresh coriander leaves.

Red Onion and Beetroot Soup

This beautiful, vivid ruby-red soup will look stunning at any dinner-party table.

INGREDIENTS

Serves 4–6

15ml/1 tbsp olive oil
350g/12oz red onions, sliced
2 garlic cloves, crushed
275g/10oz cooked beetroot, cut into sticks
1.2 litres/2 pints/5 cups vegetable stock or water
50g/2oz cooked soup pasta
30ml/2 tbsp raspberry vinegar
salt and ground black pepper
low-fat yogurt or fromage blanc, to garnish
snipped chives, to garnish

1 Heat the olive oil in a flame-proof casserole and add the onions and garlic.

2 Cook gently for 20 minutes or until the onions and garlic are soft and tender.

3 Add the beetroot, stock or water, cooked soup pasta and vinegar, and heat through. Season to taste with salt and pepper.

4 Ladle into warmed soup bowls. Top each one with a spoonful of low-fat yogurt or fromage blanc and sprinkle with chives.

Chinese-style Vegetable and Noodle Soup

This soup is wonderfully quick and easy to prepare.

INGREDIENTS

Serves 4

1.2 litres/2 pints/5 cups vegetable or chicken stock
1 garlic clove, lightly crushed
2.5cm/1in piece fresh root ginger, peeled and cut into fine matchsticks
30ml/2 tbsp soy sauce
15ml/1 tbsp cider vinegar
75g/3oz fresh shiitake or button mushrooms, stalks removed and thinly sliced
2 large spring onions, thinly sliced on the diagonal
40g/1½oz vermicelli or other fine noodles
175g/6oz Chinese leaves, shredded
a few fresh coriander leaves

1 Pour the stock into a saucepan. Add the garlic, root ginger, soy sauce and vinegar. Bring to the boil, then cover the pan and reduce the heat to very low. Leave to simmer gently for 10 minutes. Remove the garlic clove from the pan and discard.

2 Add the sliced mushrooms and spring onions and bring the soup back to the boil. Simmer for 5 minutes, uncovered, stirring occasionally. Add the noodles and shredded Chinese leaves. Simmer for 3–4 minutes, or until the noodles and vegetables are just tender. Stir in the coriander leaves. Simmer for a final 1 minute. Serve the soup hot.

Chicken Vermicelli Soup with Egg Shreds

This soup is very quick and easy – you can add all sorts of extra ingredients to vary the taste, using up leftovers such as spring onions, mushrooms, a few prawns or chopped salami.

INGREDIENTS

Serves 4–6

3 eggs
30ml/2 tbsp chopped fresh coriander or parsley
1.5 litres/2½ pints/6¼ cups good chicken stock or canned consommé
115g/4oz dried vermicelli or angel hair pasta
115g/4oz cooked chicken breast, sliced
salt and ground black pepper

1 First make the egg shreds. Whisk the eggs together in a small bowl and stir in the coriander or parsley.

2 Heat a small non-stick frying pan and pour in 30–45ml/2–3 tbsp egg, swirling to cover the base evenly. Cook until set. Repeat until all the mixture is used up.

3 Roll each pancake up and slice thinly into shreds. Set aside.

4 Bring the stock or consommé to the boil and add the pasta, breaking it up into short lengths. Cook for 3–5 minutes until the pasta is almost tender, then add the chicken, and salt and pepper to taste. Heat through for about 2–3 minutes, then stir in the egg shreds. Serve immediately.

THAI CHICKEN SOUP

To make a Thai variation, use Chinese rice noodles instead of pasta. Stir 1.5ml/½ tsp dried lemon grass, 2 small whole fresh chillies and 60ml/4 tbsp coconut milk into the stock. Add 4 sliced spring onions and plenty of chopped fresh coriander.

Parmesan and Cauliflower Soup

A silky smooth, mildly cheesy soup which isn't overpowered by the cauliflower. It makes an elegant dinner-party soup served with crisp Melba toast.

INGREDIENTS

Serves 6

1 large cauliflower
1.2 litres/2 pints/5 cups chicken or vegetable stock
175g/6oz farfalle
150ml/¼ pint/⅔ cup single cream or milk
freshly grated nutmeg
pinch of cayenne pepper
60ml/4 tbsp freshly grated Parmesan cheese
salt and ground black pepper

For the Melba toast

3–4 slices day-old white bread
freshly grated Parmesan cheese, for sprinkling
1.5ml/¼ tsp paprika

1 Cut the leaves and central stalk away from the cauliflower and discard. Divide the cauliflower into similar-size florets.

2 Bring the stock to the boil and add the cauliflower. Simmer for about 10 minutes or until very soft. Remove the cauliflower with a slotted spoon and place in a blender or food processor.

3 Add the pasta to the stock and simmer for 10 minutes until tender. Drain, reserve the pasta, and pour the liquid over the cauliflower. Add the cream or milk, nutmeg and cayenne to the cauliflower. Blend until smooth, then press through a sieve. Stir in the cooked pasta. Reheat the soup and stir in the Parmesan. Taste and adjust the seasoning if necessary.

4 Meanwhile make the Melba toast. Preheat the oven to 180°C/350°F/Gas 4. Toast the bread lightly on both sides. Quickly cut off the crusts and split each slice in half horizontally. Scrape off any doughy bits and sprinkle with Parmesan and paprika. Place on a baking sheet and bake in the oven for about 10–15 minutes or until uniformly golden. Serve with the soup.

Italian Bean and Pasta Soup

A thick and hearty soup which, followed by bread and cheese, makes a substantial lunch.

INGREDIENTS

Serves 6

175g/6oz/1½ cups dried haricot beans, soaked overnight in cold water
1.75 litres/3 pints/7½ cups chicken stock or water
115g/4oz medium pasta shells
60ml/4 tbsp olive oil, plus extra to serve
2 garlic cloves, crushed
60ml/4 tbsp chopped fresh parsley
salt and ground black pepper

1 Drain the beans and place in a large saucepan with the stock or water. Simmer, half-covered, for 2–2½ hours or until tender.

2 In a blender or food processor, process half the beans with a little of their cooking liquid, then stir into the unprocessed beans in the pan.

3 Add the pasta and simmer gently for 15 minutes until tender. (Add extra water or stock if the soup seems too thick.)

4 Heat the oil in a small pan and fry the garlic until golden. Stir into the soup with the parsley and season well with salt and pepper. Ladle into individual bowls and drizzle each with a little extra olive oil, to serve.

Courgette Soup with Small Pasta Shells

A pretty, fresh-tasting soup which could be made using cucumber instead of courgettes.

INGREDIENTS

Serves 4–6

60ml/4 tbsp olive or sunflower oil
2 onions, finely chopped
1.5 litres/2½ pints/6¼ cups chicken stock
900g/2lb courgettes
115g/4oz small soup pasta
freshly squeezed lemon juice
30ml/2 tbsp chopped fresh chervil
salt and ground black pepper
soured cream, to serve

1 Heat the oil in a large saucepan and add the onions. Cover and cook gently for about 20 minutes until very soft but not coloured, stirring occasionally.

2 Add the chicken stock to the saucepan and bring the mixture to the boil.

3 Meanwhile grate the courgettes and stir into the boiling stock with the pasta. Reduce the heat and simmer for 15 minutes until the pasta is tender. Season to taste with lemon juice, salt and pepper.

4 Stir in the chopped fresh chervil and add a swirl of soured cream before serving.

Minestrone

A substantial and popular winter soup originally from Milan, but found in various versions around the Mediterranean coasts of Italy and France. Cut the vegetables as roughly or as small as you like. Add freshly grated Parmesan cheese just before serving.

INGREDIENTS

Serves 6–8

225g/8oz/2 cups dried haricot beans
30ml/2 tbsp olive oil
50g/2oz smoked streaky bacon, diced
2 large onions, sliced
2 garlic cloves, crushed
2 carrots, diced
3 celery sticks, sliced
400g/14oz canned chopped tomatoes
2.25 litres/4 pints/10 cups beef stock
350g/12oz potatoes, diced
175g/6oz small pasta shapes, such as macaroni, stars, shells, etc
225g/8oz green cabbage, thinly sliced
175g/6oz fine green beans, sliced
115g/4oz/1 cup frozen peas
45ml/3 tbsp chopped fresh parsley
salt and ground black pepper
freshly grated Parmesan cheese, to serve

1 Cover the beans with cold water in a bowl and leave to soak overnight.

2 Heat the oil in a large saucepan and add the bacon, onions and garlic. Cover and cook gently for 5 minutes, stirring occasionally.

3 Add the carrots and celery and cook for 2–3 minutes until the vegetables are softening.

4 Drain the beans and add to the pan with the tomatoes and the beef stock. Cover and simmer for 2–2½ hours, until the beans are tender.

5 Add the potatoes 30 minutes before the soup is ready.

6 Add the pasta, cabbage, beans, peas and parsley 15 minutes before the soup is ready. Season to taste and serve with a bowl of freshly grated Parmesan cheese.

Provençal Fish Soup with Pasta

This colourful soup has all the flavours of the Mediterranean. Serve it as a main course for a deliciously filling lunch.

INGREDIENTS

Serves 4

30ml/2 tbsp olive oil
1 onion, sliced
1 garlic clove, crushed
1 leek, sliced
225g/8oz canned chopped tomatoes
pinch of Mediterranean herbs
1.5ml/¼ tsp saffron strands (optional)
115g/4oz small pasta
about 8 live mussels in the shell
450g/1lb filleted and skinned white fish, such as cod, plaice or monkfish
salt and ground black pepper

For the rouille

2 garlic cloves, crushed
1 canned pimiento, drained and chopped
15ml/1 tbsp fresh white breadcrumbs
60ml/4 tbsp mayonnaise
toasted French bread, to serve

1 Heat the oil in a large saucepan and add the onion, garlic and leek. Cover and cook gently for 5 minutes, stirring occasionally until the vegetables are soft.

2 Pour in 1 litre/1¾pints/4 cups water, the tomatoes, herbs, saffron and pasta. Season with salt and ground black pepper and cook for 15–20 minutes.

3 Scrub the mussels and pull off the "beards". Discard any that will not close when sharply tapped.

4 Cut the fish into bite-size chunks and add to the soup, placing the mussels on top. Then simmer with the lid on for 5-10 minutes until the mussels open and the fish is just cooked. Discard any unopened mussels.

5 To make the rouille, pound the garlic, canned pimiento and breadcrumbs together in a pestle and mortar (or in a blender or food processor). Stir in the mayonnaise and season well.

6 Spread the toasted French bread with the rouille and serve with the soup.

PASTA WITH FISH & SHELLFISH

Salmon Pasta with Parsley Sauce

This dish is so quick and easy to make – and delicious.

INGREDIENTS

Serves 4

450g/1lb salmon fillet, skinned
225g/8oz pasta, such as penne or twists
175g/6oz cherry tomatoes, halved
150ml/¼ pint/⅔ cup low -fat crème fraîche
45ml/3 tbsp finely chopped parsley
finely grated rind of ½ orange
salt and ground black pepper

1 Cut the salmon into bite-size pieces, arrange on a heatproof plate and cover with foil.

2 Bring a large pan of salted water to the boil, add the pasta and return to the boil. Place the plate of salmon on top and simmer for 10–12 minutes, until the pasta and salmon are cooked.

3 Drain the pasta and toss with the tomatoes and salmon. Mix together the crème fraîche, parsley, orange rind and pepper to taste, then toss into the salmon and pasta and serve hot or cold.

Tagliatelle with Saffron Mussels

Mussels in a saffron and cream sauce are served with tagliatelle in this recipe, but you can use any other pasta if you prefer.

INGREDIENTS

Serves 4

1.75kg/4–4½lb live mussels in the shell
150ml/¼ pint/⅔ cup dry white wine
2 shallots, chopped
350g/12oz dried tagliatelle
25g/1oz/2 tbsp butter
2 garlic cloves, crushed
250ml/8fl oz/1 cup double cream
generous pinch of saffron strands
1 egg yolk
salt and ground black pepper
30ml/2 tbsp chopped fresh parsley, to garnish

1 Scrub the mussels well under cold running water. Remove the "beards" and discard any mussels that are open.

2 Place the mussels in a large pan with the wine and shallots. Cover and cook over a high heat, shaking the pan occasionally, for 5-8 minutes until the mussels have opened. Drain the mussels, reserving the liquid. Discard any that remain closed. Shell all but a few of the mussels and keep warm.

3 Bring the reserved cooking liquid to the boil, then reduce by half. Strain into a jug to remove any grit.

4 Cook the tagliatelle in plenty of boiling salted water for about 10 minutes, until *al dente.*

5 Meanwhile, melt the butter and fry the garlic for 1 minute. Pour in the mussel liquid, cream and saffron strands. Heat gently until the sauce thickens slightly. Off the heat, stir in the egg yolk, shelled mussels, and season.

6 Drain the tagliatelle and transfer to warmed serving bowls. Spoon the sauce over and sprinkle with chopped parsley. Garnish with the mussels in shells and serve at once.

Spaghetti with Tomato and Clam Sauce

Small sweet clams make this a delicately succulent sauce. Cockles would make a good substitute, or even mussels, but don't be tempted to use seafood pickled in vinegar.

INGREDIENTS

Serves 4

900g/2lb live small clams in the shell, or 2 x 400g/14oz cans clams in brine, drained
90ml/6 tbsp olive oil
2 garlic cloves, crushed
500g/1¼lb canned chopped tomatoes
45ml/3 tbsp chopped fresh parsley
450g/1lb spaghetti
salt and ground black pepper

1 If using live clams, place them in a bowl of cold water and rinse several times to remove any grit or sand, then drain well.

2 Heat the oil in a saucepan and add the clams. Stir over a high heat until the clams open. Discard any that do not open. Transfer the clams to a bowl with a slotted spoon and set aside.

3 Reduce the clam juice left in the pan to almost nothing by boiling fast. Add the garlic and fry until golden. Pour in the tomatoes, bring to the boil and cook for 3–4 minutes until reduced. Stir in the clam mixture or canned clams and half the parsley and heat through. Season to taste.

4 Cook the pasta in plenty of boiling salted water according to the instructions on the packet. Drain well and turn into a warm serving dish. Pour over the sauce and sprinkle with the remaining chopped parsley.

Spaghetti with Clams

Try chopped fresh dill for a delicious alternative in this dish.

INGREDIENTS

Serves 4

24 live clams in the shell, scrubbed
250ml/8fl oz/1 cup water
120ml/4fl oz/½ cup dry white wine
450g/1lb spaghetti, preferably Italian
75ml/5 tbsp olive oil
2 garlic cloves, minced
45ml/3 tbsp chopped fresh parsley
salt and ground black pepper

1 Rinse the clams well in cold water and drain. Place in a large saucepan with the water and wine and bring to the boil. Cover and steam until the shells open, about 6–8 minutes.

2 Discard any clams that have not opened. Remove the clams from their shells. If large, chop them roughly.

3 Strain the cooking liquid through a strainer lined with muslin. Place in a small saucepan and boil rapidly until reduced by about half. Set aside.

4 Cook the spaghetti in plenty of boiling salted water according to the instructions on the packet until *al dente*.

5 Meanwhile, heat the olive oil in a large frying pan. Add the garlic and cook for 2–3 minutes, but do not let it brown. Add the reduced clam liquid and the parsley. Cook over a low heat until the spaghetti is ready.

6 Drain the spaghetti. Add to the frying pan, increase the heat to medium, and add the clams. Cook for 3–4 minutes, stirring, to coat the spaghetti with the sauce and to heat the clams.

7 Season with salt and pepper and serve at once.

Pasta with Tuna, Capers and Anchovies

This piquant sauce could be made without the addition of tomatoes – just heat the oil, add the other ingredients and heat through gently before tossing with the pasta.

INGREDIENTS

Serves 4

400g/14oz can tuna fish in oil
30ml/2 tbsp olive oil
2 garlic cloves, crushed
800g/1¾lb canned chopped tomatoes
6 canned anchovy fillets, drained
30ml/2 tbsp capers in vinegar, drained
30ml/2 tbsp chopped fresh basil
450g/1lb rigatoni, penne or garganelle
salt and ground black pepper
fresh basil sprigs, to garnish

1 Drain the oil from the can of tuna fish into a large saucepan, add the olive oil and heat gently until the oil mixture stops spitting.

2 Add the garlic and fry until golden. Stir in the tomatoes and simmer for about 25 minutes until thickened.

3 Flake the tuna and cut the anchovies in half. Stir into the sauce with the capers and chopped basil. Season well.

4 Cook the pasta in plenty of boiling salted water according to the instructions on the packet. Drain well and toss with the sauce. Garnish with fresh basil sprigs.

Noodles with Prawns in Lemon Sauce

As in many Chinese dishes the fish is here purely for colour and flavour.

INGREDIENTS

Serves 4

2 packets Chinese egg noodles
15ml/1 tbsp sunflower oil
2 celery sticks, cut into matchsticks
2 garlic cloves, crushed
4 spring onions, sliced
2 carrots, cut into matchsticks
7.5cm/3in piece cucumber, cut into matchsticks
115g/4oz prawns in the shells
1 lemon
30ml/2 tbsp lemon juice or sauce
5ml/1 tsp cornflour
60–75ml/4–5 tbsp fish stock
115g/4oz/1 cup shelled prawns
salt and ground black pepper
a few sprigs dill, to garnish

1 Put the noodles in boiling water and leave to soak as directed on the packet. Meanwhile, heat the oil in a pan and stir-fry the celery, garlic, spring onions and carrots for 2–3 minutes.

2 Add the cucumber and whole prawns and cook for about 2–3 minutes. Meanwhile, peel the rind from the lemon and cut into long thin shreds. Place in boiling water for 1 minute.

3 Blend the lemon juice, or lemon sauce, with the cornflour and stock and add to the pan. Bring gently to the boil, stirring, and cook for 1 minute.

4 Stir in the shelled prawns, the drained lemon rind and seasoning to taste. Drain the noodles and serve with the prawns, garnished with dill.

COOK'S TIP

These noodles can be deep-fried. Cook as above; drain on kitchen paper. Deep-fry in batches until golden and crisp.

Seafood Pasta Shells with Spinach Sauce

You'll need very large pasta shells, measuring about 4cm/1½in long for this dish; don't try stuffing smaller shells – they will be much too fiddly!

INGREDIENTS

Serves 4

- 15g/½oz/1 tbsp margarine
- 8 spring onions, finely sliced
- 6 tomatoes
- 32 large dried pasta shells
- 225g/8oz/1 cup low-fat soft cheese
- 90ml/6 tbsp skimmed milk
- pinch of freshly grated nutmeg
- 225g/8oz/2 cups prawns
- 175g/6oz can white crab meat, drained and flaked
- 115g/4oz frozen chopped spinach, thawed and drained
- salt and ground black pepper

1 Preheat the oven to 150°C/300°F/Gas 2. Melt the margarine in a small saucepan and gently cook the spring onions for 3–4 minutes, or until softened.

2 Slash the bottoms of the tomatoes, plunge into a saucepan of boiling water for 45 seconds, then into a saucepan of cold water. Slip off the skins. Halve the tomatoes, remove the seeds and cores and roughly chop the flesh.

3 Cook the pasta shells in plenty of boiling salted water for about 10 minutes, or until *al dente*. Drain well.

4 Heat the soft cheese and milk in a saucepan, stirring until blended. Season with salt, pepper and nutmeg. Measure 30ml/2 tbsp of the sauce into a bowl.

5 Add the spring onions, tomatoes, prawns, and crab meat to the bowl. Mix well. Spoon the filling into the shells and place in a single layer in a shallow ovenproof dish. Cover with foil and cook in the preheated oven for 10 minutes.

6 Stir the spinach into the remaining sauce. Bring to the boil and simmer gently for 1 minute, stirring all the time. Drizzle over the pasta shells and serve hot.

Pasta Bows with Smoked Salmon and Dill

In Italy, pasta cooked with smoked salmon is very fashionable. This is a quick and luxurious sauce.

INGREDIENTS

Serves 4

6 spring onions
50g/2oz/4 tbsp butter
90ml/6 tbsp dry white wine or vermouth
450ml/¾ pint/1¾ cups double cream
freshly grated nutmeg
225g/8oz smoked salmon
30ml/2 tbsp chopped fresh dill or 15ml/1 tbsp dried
freshly squeezed lemon juice
450g/1lb farfalle
salt and ground black pepper

1 Slice the spring onions finely. Melt the butter in a saucepan and gently fry the spring onions for 1 minute until softened.

2 Add the wine or vermouth and boil hard to reduce to about 30ml/2 tbsp. Stir in the cream and add salt, pepper and nutmeg to taste. Bring to the boil and simmer for 2–3 minutes until the sauce is slightly thickened.

3 Cut the smoked salmon into 2.5cm/1in squares and stir into the sauce with the dill. Taste and add a little lemon juice. Keep the sauce warm.

4 Cook the pasta in plenty of boiling salted water according to the instructions on the packet. Drain well. Toss the pasta with the sauce and serve immediately.

Spaghetti with Mixed Shellfish Sauce

A special occasion sauce for an evening of entertaining is just what this is, so serve it in bountiful portions to your guests.

INGREDIENTS

Serves 4

50g/2oz/4 tbsp butter
2 shallots, chopped
2 garlic cloves, chopped
350g/12oz spaghetti
2 tbsp finely chopped fresh basil
300ml/½ pint/1¼ cups dry white wine
450g/1lb mussels, scrubbed
115g/4oz squid, washed
5ml/1 tsp chilli powder
350g/12oz raw peeled prawns
300ml/½ pint/1¼ cups soured cream
salt and ground black pepper
50g/2oz/⅓ cup Parmesan cheese, freshly grated
chopped fresh flat leaf parsley, to garnish

1 Melt half the butter in a frying pan and fry 1 shallot and 1 garlic clove for about 5 minutes until softened

2 Cook the pasta in plenty of boiling salted water according to the instructions on the packet.

3 Stir in half the basil and the wine and bring to the boil.

4 Discard any mussels that are open and do not shut when tapped with the back of a knife. Quickly add the remaining mussels to the pan, cover and simmer for about 5 minutes until all the shells have opened. Discard any mussels that do not open. Using a slotted spoon, transfer the mussels to a plate, remove them from their shells and return to the pan. Reserve a few mussels in the shells for garnishing.

5 Meanwhile, slice the squid into thin circles. Melt the remaining butter in a frying pan and fry the remaining shallot and garlic for about 5 minutes until softened.

6 Add the remaining basil, the squid, chilli powder and prawns to the pan and stir-fry for 5 minutes until the prawns have turned pink and tender.

7 Turn the mussel mixture into the prawn mixture and bring to the boil. Stir in the soured cream and season to taste. Bring almost to the boil and simmer for 1 minute.

8 Drain the pasta thoroughly and stir it into the sauce with the Parmesan cheese until well coated. Serve immediately, garnished with chopped flat leaf parsley and the reserved mussels in their shells.

Pasta with Spinach and Anchovy Sauce

Deliciously earthy, this would make a good starter or light supper dish. Add some sultanas to the sauce to ring the changes.

INGREDIENTS

Serves 4

900g/2lb fresh spinach or 500g/1¼lb frozen leaf spinach, thawed
450g/1lb angel hair pasta
salt, to taste
60ml/4 tbsp olive oil
45ml/3 tbsp pine nuts
2 garlic cloves
6 canned anchovy fillets, drained and chopped, or whole salted anchovies, rinsed, boned and chopped
butter, for tossing the pasta

1 If using fresh spinach, wash it well and remove any tough stalks. Drain thoroughly. Place in a large saucepan with only the water that clings to the leaves. Cover with a lid and cook over a high heat, shaking the pan occasionally, until the spinach is just wilted and still bright green. Drain.

2 Cook the pasta in plenty of boiling salted water according to the instructions on the packet.

3 Heat the oil in a saucepan and fry the pine nuts until golden. Remove with a slotted spoon. Add the garlic to the oil in the pan and fry until golden. Add the chopped anchovies to the pan.

4 Stir in the spinach and cook for 2–3 minutes or until heated through. Stir in the pine nuts. Drain the pasta, toss in a little butter and turn into a warmed serving dish. Top with the hot sauce and fork through roughly before serving.

Tagliatelle with Haddock and Avocado

You will need to start this recipe the day before because the haddock should be left to marinate overnight.

INGREDIENTS

Serves 4

350g/12oz fresh haddock fillets, skinned
2.5ml/½ tsp each ground cumin, ground coriander and turmeric
150ml/¼ pint/⅔ cup fromage frais
150ml/¼ pint/⅔ cup double cream
15ml/1 tbsp lemon juice
25g/1oz/2 tbsp butter
1 onion, chopped
15ml/1 tbsp plain flour
150ml/¼ pint/⅔ cup fish stock
350g/12oz tagliatelle
1 avocado, peeled, stoned and sliced
2 tomatoes, seeded and chopped
salt and ground black pepper
fresh rosemary sprigs, to garnish

1 Carefully cut the haddock into bite-size pieces.

2 Mix together all the spices, seasoning, fromage frais, cream and lemon juice.

3 Stir in the haddock to coat. Cover the dish and leave to marinate overnight.

4 Heat the butter in a frying pan and fry the onion for about 10 minutes until softened. Stir in the flour, then blend in the stock until smooth.

5 Carefully stir in the haddock mixture until well blended. Bring to the boil, stirring, cover and simmer for about 30 seconds. Remove from the heat.

6 Meanwhile, cook the pasta in plenty of boiling salted water according to the instructions on the packet.

7 Stir the avocado and tomatoes into the haddock mixture.

8 Drain the pasta thoroughly and divide among four serving plates. Spoon over the sauce and serve immediately, garnished with fresh rosemary.

Smoked Trout Cannelloni

Smoked trout can be bought already filleted or whole. If you buy fillets, you'll need 225g/8oz.

INGREDIENTS

Serves 4–6

1 large onion, finely chopped
1 garlic clove, crushed
60ml/4 tbsp vegetable stock
2 x 400g/14oz cans chopped tomatoes
2.5ml/½ tsp dried mixed herbs
1 smoked trout, about 400g/14oz
75g/3oz/¾ cup frozen peas, thawed
75g/3oz/1½ cups fresh breadcrumbs
16 cannelloni tubes
salt and ground black pepper
mixed salad, to serve (optional)
25ml/1½ tbsp freshly grated Parmesan cheese

For the cheese sauce
25g/1oz/2 tbsp margarine
25g/1oz/¼ cup plain flour
350ml/12fl oz/1½ cups skimmed milk
freshly grated nutmeg

1 Simmer the onion, garlic and stock in a large covered saucepan for 3 minutes. Uncover and continue to cook, stirring occasionally, until the stock has reduced entirely.

2 Stir in the tomatoes and dried herbs. Simmer, uncovered, for a further 10 minutes, or until the mixture is very thick.

3 Meanwhile, skin the smoked trout with a sharp knife. Carefully flake the flesh and discard the bones. Mix the fish together with the tomato mixture, peas, breadcrumbs, salt and ground black pepper.

4 Preheat the oven to 190°C/375°F/Gas 5. Spoon the filling into the cannelloni tubes and arrange in an ovenproof dish.

5 For the sauce, put the margarine, flour and milk into a saucepan and cook over a medium heat, whisking constantly until the sauce thickens. Simmer for 2–3 minutes, stirring all the time. Season to taste with salt, pepper and nutmeg.

6 Pour the sauce over the cannelloni and sprinkle with the grated Parmesan cheese. Bake in the oven for 35–40 minutes, or until the top is golden and bubbling. Serve with a mixed salad, if desired.

Pasta with Scallops and Tomato Sauce

Fresh basil gives this sauce a distinctive flavour.

INGREDIENTS

Serves 4

450g/1lb pasta, such as fettucine or linguine
30ml/2 tbsp olive oil
2 garlic cloves, crushed
450g/1lb sea scallops, halved horizontally
salt and ground black pepper
30ml/2 tbsp chopped fresh basil

For the sauce

30ml/2 tbsp olive oil
½ onion, minced
1 garlic clove, crushed
2.5ml/½ tsp salt
2 x 400g/14oz cans plum tomatoes

1 For the sauce, heat the oil in a non-stick frying pan. Add the onion, garlic and a little salt, and cook over a medium heat for about 5 minutes until just softened, stirring occasionally.

2 Add the tomatoes, with their juice, and crush with a fork. Bring to the boil, then reduce the heat and simmer gently for 15 minutes. Remove from the heat and set aside.

3 Cook the pasta in plenty of boiling salted water, according to the instructions on the packet, until *al dente*.

4 Meanwhile, combine the oil and garlic in another non-stick frying pan and cook until just sizzling, about 30 seconds. Add the scallops and 2.5ml/½ tsp salt and cook over a high heat, tossing until the scallops are cooked through, about 3 minutes.

5 Add the scallops to the tomato sauce. Season with salt and pepper, stir and keep warm.

6 Drain the pasta, rinse under hot water and drain again. Place in a large serving dish. Add the sauce and the basil and toss thoroughly. Serve immediately.

Baked Seafood Spaghetti

In this dish, each portion is baked and served in an individual packet which is then opened at the table. Use baking parchment paper or foil to make the packets.

INGREDIENTS

Serves 4

450g/1lb fresh mussels
120ml/4fl oz/½ cup dry white wine
60ml/4 tbsp olive oil
2 garlic cloves, finely chopped
450g/1lb tomatoes, fresh or canned, peeled and finely chopped
400g/14oz spaghetti or other long pasta
225g/8oz/2 cups peeled and deveined prawns, fresh or frozen
30ml/2 tbsp chopped fresh parsley
salt and ground black pepper

1 Scrub the mussels well under cold running water, cutting off the "beards" with a small sharp knife. Discard any that do not close when tapped sharply. Place the mussels and the wine in a large saucepan and heat until opened.

2 Lift out the mussels and remove to a side dish. Discard any that do not open. Strain the cooking liquid into a bowl through kitchen paper and reserve until needed. Preheat the oven to 150°C/300°F/Gas 2.

3 In a medium saucepan, heat the oil and garlic together for 1–2 minutes. Add the tomatoes and cook over a moderate to high heat until softened. Stir 175ml/6fl oz/¾ cup of the mussel cooking liquid into the saucepan.

4 Cook the pasta in plenty of boiling salted water until just *al dente*. Just before draining the pasta, add the prawns and parsley to the tomato sauce. Cook for 2 minutes. Taste for seasoning, adding salt and pepper if necessary. Remove from the heat.

5 Prepare four pieces of baking parchment paper or foil about 30 × 45cm/12 × 18in. Place each sheet in the centre of a shallow bowl. Turn the drained pasta into a mixing bowl. Add the tomato sauce and mix well. Stir in the mussels.

6 Divide the pasta and seafood among the four pieces of paper or foil, placing a mound in the centre of each, and twisting the ends together to make a closed packet. Arrange on a large baking sheet and place in the centre of the oven. Bake for 8–10 minutes. Place the unopened packets on individual serving plates.

Fusilli with Vegetable and Prawn Sauce

You will need to start this recipe the day before because the prawns should be left to marinate overnight.

INGREDIENTS

Serves 4

450g/1lb/4 cups peeled prawns
60ml/4 tbsp soy sauce
45ml/3 tbsp olive oil
350g/12oz curly spaghetti (fusilli col buco)
1 yellow pepper, cored, seeded and cut into strips
225g/8oz broccoli florets
1 bunch spring onions, shredded
2.5cm/1in piece fresh ginger root, peeled and shredded
15ml/1 tbsp chopped fresh oregano
30ml/2 tbsp dry sherry
15ml/1 tbsp cornflour
300ml/½ pint/1¼ cups fish stock
salt and ground black pepper

1 Place the prawns in a mixing bowl. Stir in half the soy sauce and 30ml/2 tbsp of the olive oil. Cover and marinate overnight.

2 Cook the pasta in plenty of boiling salted water according to the instructions on the packet.

3 Meanwhile, heat the remaining oil in a wok or frying pan and fry the prawns for 1 minute.

4 Add the pepper, broccoli, spring onions, ginger and oregano and stir-fry for about 1–2 minutes.

5 Drain the pasta thoroughly, set aside and keep warm. Meanwhile, blend together the sherry and cornflour until smooth. Stir in the stock and remaining soy sauce until well blended.

6 Pour the sauce into the wok or pan, bring to the boil and stir-fry for 2 minutes until thickened. Pour over the pasta and serve.

Tuna Lasagne

INGREDIENTS

Serves 6

1 quantity fresh pasta dough, cut for lasagne, or 375g/12oz no-precook dried lasagne
15g/½oz butter
1 small onion, finely chopped
1 garlic clove, finely chopped
115g/4oz mushrooms, thinly sliced
60ml/4 tbsp dry white wine (optional)
600ml/1 pint/2½ cups white sauce
150ml/¼ pint/⅔ cup whipping cream
45ml/3 tbsp chopped parsley
2 x 200g/7oz cans tuna, drained
2 canned pimientos, cut into strips
65g/2½oz/generous ½ cup frozen peas, thawed
115g/4oz mozzarella cheese, grated
30ml/2 tbsp freshly grated Parmesan cheese
salt and ground black pepper

1 For fresh lasagne, bring a large pan of salted water to the boil. Cook the lasagne, in small batches, until almost tender to the bite. For dried lasagne, soak in a bowl of hot water for 3–5 minutes.

2 Place the lasagne in a colander and rinse with cold water. Lay on a dish towel to drain.

3 Preheat the oven to 180°C/350°F//Gas 4. Melt the butter in a saucepan and cook the onion until soft.

4 Add the garlic and mushrooms, and cook until soft, stirring occasionally. Pour in the wine, if using. Boil for 1 minute. Add the white sauce, cream and parsley. Season.

5 Spoon a thin layer of sauce over the base of a 30 × 23cm/12 × 9in baking dish. Cover with a layer of lasagne sheets.

6 Flake the tuna. Scatter half the tuna, pimiento strips, peas and mozzarella over the lasagne. Spoon one-third of the remaining sauce over the top, cover with another layer of lasagne sheets.

7 Repeat the layers, ending with pasta and sauce. Sprinkle with the Parmesan. Bake for 30–40 minutes or until lightly browned.

Pasta Tubes with Tuna and Olive Sauce

This colourful sauce combines well with a thicker and shorter pasta.

INGREDIENTS

Serves 4

350g/12oz rigatoni
30ml/2 tbsp olive oil
1 onion, chopped
2 garlic cloves, chopped
400g/14oz can chopped tomatoes
50g/2oz/4 tbsp tomato purée
50g/2oz/½ cup stoned black olives, quartered
15ml/1 tbsp chopped fresh oregano
225g/8oz can tuna in oil, drained and flaked
2.5ml/½ tsp anchovy purée
15ml/1 tbsp capers, rinsed
115g/4oz/1 cup grated Cheddar cheese
45ml/3 tbsp fresh white breadcrumbs
salt and ground black pepper
flat leaf parsley sprigs, to garnish

1 Cook the pasta in plenty of boiling salted water according to the instructions on the packet.

2 Meanwhile, heat the oil in a frying pan and fry the onion and garlic for about 10 minutes until softened.

3 Add the tomatoes, tomato purée, and salt and pepper, and bring to the boil. Simmer gently for 5 minutes, stirring occasionally.

4 Stir in the olives, oregano, tuna, anchovy purée and capers. Spoon the mixture into a mixing bowl.

5 Drain the pasta, toss well in the sauce and spoon into flameproof serving dishes.

6 Preheat the grill and sprinkle the cheese and breadcrumbs over the pasta. Grill for about 10 minutes until the pasta is heated through and the cheese has melted. Serve at once, garnished with flat leaf parsley.

Spaghetti with Hot-and-sour Fish

A truly Chinese spicy taste is what makes this sauce so different.

INGREDIENTS

Serves 4

350g/12oz spaghetti
450g/1lb monkfish, skinned
225g/8oz courgettes
1 green chilli, cored and seeded (optional)
15ml/1 tbsp olive oil
1 large onion, chopped
5ml/1 tsp turmeric
115g/4oz/1 cup shelled peas, thawed if frozen
10ml/2 tsp lemon juice
75ml/5 tbsp hoisin sauce
150ml/¼ pint/⅔ cup water
salt and ground black pepper
fresh dill sprig, to garnish

1 Cook the pasta in plenty of boiling salted water according to the instructions on the packet.

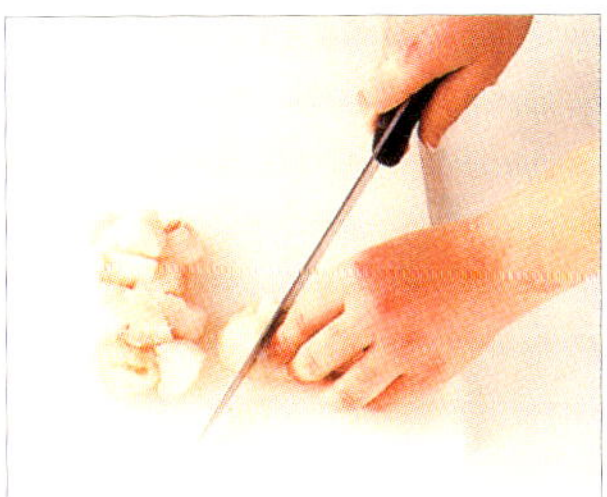

2 Cut the monkfish into bite-size pieces. Thinly slice the courgettes, then finely chop the chilli, if using.

3 Heat the oil in a large frying pan and fry the onion for 5 minutes until softened. Add the turmeric.

4 Add the chilli, if using, courgettes and peas, and fry over a medium heat for 5 minutes until the vegetables have softened.

5 Stir in the fish, lemon juice, hoisin sauce and water. Bring to the boil, then simmer, uncovered, for about 5 minutes or until the fish is tender. Season.

6 Drain the pasta thoroughly and turn into a serving dish. Toss in the sauce to coat. Serve at once, garnished with fresh dill.

Saffron Pappardelle

A wonderful dish with a delicious shellfish sauce.

INGREDIENTS

Serves 4

large pinch saffron strands
4 sun-dried tomatoes, chopped
5ml/1 tsp fresh thyme
12 large prawns in their shells
225g/8oz baby squid
225g/8oz monkfish fillet
2–3 garlic cloves
2 small onions, quartered
1 small bulb fennel, trimmed and sliced
150ml/¼ pint/⅔ cup white wine
225g/8oz pappardelle
salt and ground black pepper
30ml/2 tbsp chopped fresh parsley, to garnish

1 Put the saffron, sun-dried tomatoes and thyme into a bowl with 60ml/4 tbsp hot water. Leave to soak for 30 minutes.

2 Wash the prawns and carefully remove the shells, leaving the heads and tails intact. Pull the body from the squid and remove the quill. Cut the tentacles from the head and rinse under cold water. Pull off the outer skin and cut into 5mm/¼in rings. Cut the monkfish into 2.5cm/1in cubes.

3 Put the garlic, onions and fennel into a pan with the wine. Cover and simmer for 5 minutes until tender.

4 Add the monkfish, saffron, tomatoes and thyme in their liquid. Cover and cook for 3 minutes. Then add the prawns and squid. Cover and cook gently for 1–2 minutes (do not overcook or the squid will become tough).

5 Meanwhile, cook the pasta in a large pan of boiling, salted water until *al dente*. Drain thoroughly.

6 Divide the pasta among four serving dishes and top with the fish and shellfish sauce. Sprinkle with parsley and serve at once.

Black Pasta with Scallops

A stunning pasta dish using black tagliatelle.

INGREDIENTS

Serves 4

120ml/4fl oz/½ cup low-fat crème fraîche
10ml/2 tsp wholegrain mustard
2 garlic cloves, crushed
30–45ml/2–3 tbsp fresh lime juice
60ml/4 tbsp chopped fresh parsley
30ml/2 tbsp snipped chives
350g/12oz black tagliatelle
12 large scallops
60ml/4 tbsp white wine
150ml/¼ pint/⅔ cup fish stock
salt and ground black pepper
lime wedges and parsley sprigs, to garnish

1 To make the tartare sauce, mix the crème fraîche, mustard, garlic, lime juice, herbs and seasoning together in a bowl.

2 Cook the pasta in a large pan of boiling, salted water until *al dente*. Drain thoroughly.

3 Slice the scallops in half horizontally. Keep any coral whole. Put the white wine and fish stock into a saucepan and heat to simmering point. Add the scallops and cook very gently for 3–4 minutes (no longer or they will become tough).

4 Remove the scallops. Boil the wine and stock to reduce by half and add the green sauce to the pan. Heat gently to warm, replace the scallops and cook gently for 1 minute. Spoon over the pasta and garnish with lime wedges and sprigs of parsley.

Fried Singapore Noodles

Thai fishcakes vary in their size and their spiciness. They are available from Oriental supermarkets.

INGREDIENTS

Serves 4

175g/6oz rice noodles
60ml/4 tbsp vegetable oil
2.5ml/½ tsp salt
75g/3oz/¾ cup cooked prawns
175g/6oz cooked pork, cut into matchsticks
1 green pepper, seeded and cut into matchsticks
2.5ml/½ tsp sugar
10ml/2 tsp curry powder
75g/3oz Thai fishcakes
10ml/2 tsp dark soy sauce

1 Soak the rice noodles in water for about 10 minutes, drain well through a colander, then pat dry with kitchen paper.

2 Heat a wok, then add half the oil. When the oil is hot, add the noodles and salt and stir-fry for 2 minutes. Transfer to a warmed serving dish and keep warm.

3 Heat the remaining oil and add the prawns, pork, pepper, sugar, curry powder and remaining salt. Stir-fry for 1 minute.

4 Return the noodles to the pan and stir-fry with the Thai fishcakes for 2 minutes. Stir in the soy sauce and serve immediately.

Mixed Rice Noodles

A delicious noodle dish made extra special by adding avocado and garnishing with prawns.

INGREDIENTS

Serves 4

15ml/1 tbsp sunflower oil
2.5cm/1in piece fresh root ginger, peeled and grated
2 garlic cloves, crushed
45ml/3 tbsp dark soy sauce
150ml/¼ pint/⅔ cup boiling water
225g/8oz/2 cups peas, thawed if frozen
450g/1lb rice noodles
450g/1lb fresh spinach, coarse stalks removed
30ml/2 tbsp smooth peanut butter
30ml/2 tbsp tahini paste
150ml/¼ pint/⅔ cup milk
1 ripe avocado, peeled and stoned
roasted peanuts and peeled prawns, to garnish

1 Heat a wok, then add the oil. When the oil is hot, stir-fry the ginger and garlic for 30 seconds. Add 15ml/1 tbsp of the soy sauce and the boiling water.

2 Add the peas and noodles, then cook for 3 minutes. Stir in the spinach. Remove the vegetables and noodles, drain well and keep warm.

3 Stir the smooth peanut butter, remaining soy sauce, tahini paste and milk together in the wok, and simmer for 1 minute.

4 Add the vegetables and noodles, slice in the avocado and toss together. Serve piled on individual plates. Spoon some sauce over each portion and garnish with peanuts and prawns.

Pasta with Prawns and Feta Cheese

This dish combines the richness of fresh prawns with the tartness of feta cheese. Goat's cheese could also be used, if preferred.

INGREDIENTS

Serves 4

450g/1lb raw prawns in the shell
6 spring onions
225g/8oz feta cheese
50g/2oz/4 tbsp butter
small bunch fresh chives
450g/1lb penne, garganelle or rigatoni
salt and ground black pepper

COOK'S TIP

If fresh prawns are not available, use well-thawed frozen, and add to the sauce at the last minute together with the spring onions.

1 Remove the heads from the prawns by twisting and pulling off. Peel the prawns and discard the shells.

2 On a nylon chopping board, chop the spring onions and the feta cheese using a sharp knife.

3 Melt the butter in a frying pan and stir in the prawns. When they turn pink, add the spring onions and cook gently over a low heat for about 1 minute.

4 Stir the feta cheese into the prawn mixture and season with black pepper.

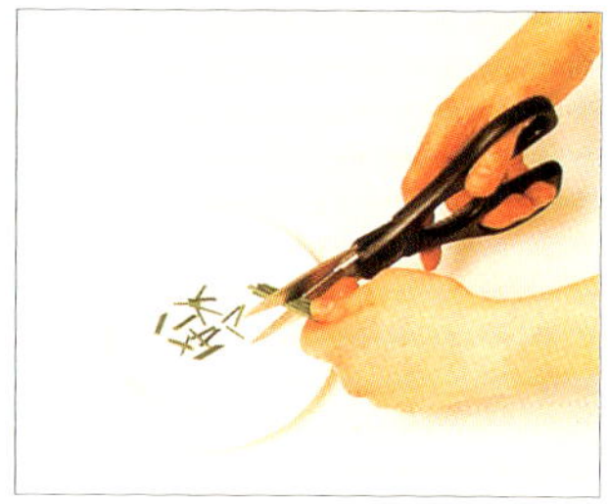

5 Snip the chives into 2.5cm/1in lengths and stir half into the prawn mixture.

6 Cook the pasta in plenty of boiling salted water according to the instructions on the packet. Drain well, pile into a warmed serving dish and top with the sauce. Scatter with the remaining chives and serve.

Tagliatelle with Smoked Salmon

This is a pretty pasta dish with the light texture of the cucumber complementing the fish perfectly.

INGREDIENTS

Serves 4

350g/12oz tagliatelle
½ cucumber
75g/3oz/6 tbsp butter
grated rind of 1 orange
30ml/2 tbsp chopped fresh dill
300ml/½ pint/1¼ cups single cream
15ml/1 tbsp orange juice
115g/4oz smoked salmon, skinned
salt and ground black pepper

1 Cook the pasta in plenty of boiling salted water according to the instructions on the packet.

2 Using a sharp knife, cut the cucumber in half lengthways then, using a small spoon, scoop out the seeds and discard.

3 Turn the cucumber on the flat side and slice thinly.

4 Melt the butter in a saucepan, add the orange rind and dill and stir well. Add the cucumber and cook gently for 2 minutes, stirring occasionally.

5 Add the cream and orange juice, and season to taste. Then simmer for 1 minute.

6 Meanwhile, cut the salmon into thin strips. Stir into the sauce and heat through.

7 Drain the pasta thoroughly and toss in the sauce until well coated. Serve immediately.

Mixed Summer Pasta

A pretty and colourful sauce with bags of flavour makes this a popular dish for the summer.

INGREDIENTS

Serves 4

115g/4oz French beans, cut into 2.5cm/1in pieces
350g/12oz curly spaghetti (fusilli col buco)
30ml/2 tbsp olive oil
½ fennel bulb, sliced
1 bunch spring onions, sliced diagonally
115g/4oz yellow cherry tomatoes
115g/4oz red cherry tomatoes
30ml/2 tbsp chopped fresh dill
225g/8oz/2 cups peeled prawns
15ml/1 tbsp lemon juice
15ml/1 tbsp wholegrain mustard
60ml/4 tbsp soured cream
salt and ground black pepper
fresh dill sprigs, to garnish

1 Cook the beans in a saucepan of boiling salted water for about 5 minutes until tender. Drain through a colander.

2 Cook the pasta in plenty of boiling salted water, according to the instructions on the packet, until *al dente*.

3 Heat the oil in a frying pan and fry the sliced fennel and spring onions for about 5 minutes.

4 Stir in all the cherry tomatoes and fry for a further 5 minutes, stirring occasionally.

5 Add the dill and prawns and cook for 1 minute.

6 Stir in the lemon juice, wholegrain mustard, soured cream, seasoning and beans and simmer for 1 minute.

7 Drain the pasta and toss with the sauce. Serve immediately, garnished with fresh dill.

Spaghetti with Mussels

Mussels are popular in all the coastal regions of Italy, and are delicious with pasta. This simple dish is greatly improved by using the freshest mussels available.

INGREDIENTS

Serves 4

900g/2lb fresh mussels, in the shell
75ml/5 tbsp olive oil
3 garlic cloves, finely chopped
60ml/4 tbsp chopped fresh parsley
60ml/4 tbsp white wine
400g/14oz spaghetti
salt and ground black pepper

1 Scrub the mussels well under cold running water, carefully cutting off the "beards" with a small sharp knife. Discard any that do not close when tapped sharply.

COOK'S TIP

Mussels should be firmly closed when fresh. If a mussel is slightly open, pinch it closed. If it remains closed on its own, it is alive. If it remains open, discard it. Fresh mussels should be consumed as soon as possible after being purchased. They may be kept in a bowl of cold water in the fridge.

2 Place the mussels with a cupful of water in a large saucepan over a moderate heat. As soon as they open, lift them out one by one with a slotted spoon.

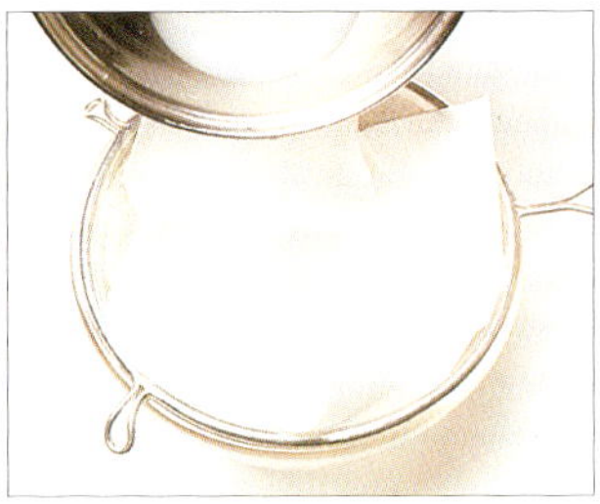

3 When all the mussels have opened (discard any that do not), strain the liquid in the saucepan through a layer of kitchen paper to remove any grit, and reserve until needed.

4 Heat the oil in a large frying pan. Add the garlic and parsley, and cook for 2–3 minutes. Add the mussels, their cooking liquid and the wine. Cook over a moderate heat until heated through.

5 Add a generous amount of pepper to the sauce. Taste for seasoning; add salt if necessary.

6 Cook the pasta in plenty of boiling salted water until *al dente*. Drain, then tip it into the frying pan with the sauce, and stir well over a moderate heat for 3–4 minutes. Serve at once.

Spaghetti with Seafood Sauce

The Italian name for this tomato-based sauce is marinara.

INGREDIENTS

Serves 4

45ml/3 tbsp olive oil
1 onion, chopped
1 garlic clove, finely chopped
225g/8oz spaghetti
600ml/1 pint/2½ cups passata
15ml/1 tbsp tomato purée
5ml/1 tsp dried oregano
1 bay leaf
5ml/1 tsp sugar
115g/4oz/1 cup cooked peeled shrimps (rinsed well if canned)
115g/4oz/1 cup cooked peeled prawns
175g/6oz/1½ cups cooked clam or cockle meat (rinsed well if canned or bottled)
15ml/1 tbsp lemon juice
45ml/3 tbsp chopped fresh parsley
25g/1oz/2 tbsp butter
salt and ground black pepper
4 whole cooked prawns, to garnish

1 Heat the oil in a pan and add the onion and garlic. Fry over a moderate heat for 6–7 minutes, until the onions have softened.

2 Meanwhile, cook the spaghetti in a large saucepan of boiling salted water for 10–12 minutes until *al dente*.

3 Stir the passata, tomato purée, oregano, bay leaf and sugar into the onions and season well. Bring to the boil, then simmer for 2–3 minutes.

4 Add the shellfish, lemon juice and 30ml/2 tbsp of the parsley. Stir well, then cover and cook for 6–7 minutes.

5 Meanwhile, drain the spaghetti when it is ready and add the butter to the pan. Return the drained spaghetti to the pan and toss in the butter. Season well.

6 Divide the spaghetti among four warmed plates and top with the seafood sauce. Sprinkle with the remaining chopped parsley, garnish with whole prawns and serve immediately.

Pasta with Fresh Sardine Sauce

In this classic Sicilian dish, fresh sardines are combined with raisins and pine nuts.

INGREDIENTS

Serves 4

30g/1¼oz/3 tbsp sultanas
450g/1lb fresh sardines
90ml/6 tbsp breadcrumbs
1 small fennel bulb
90ml/6 tbsp olive oil
1 onion, very thinly sliced
30g/1¼oz/3 tbsp pine nuts
2.5ml/½ tsp fennel seeds
400g/14oz long hollow pasta, such as percatelli, zite or bucatini
salt and ground black pepper

1 Soak the sultanas in warm water for 15 minutes. Drain and pat dry.

2 Clean the sardines. Open each one out flat and remove the central bones and head. Wash well and shake dry. Sprinkle evenly with the breadcrumbs.

3 Coarsely chop the top fronds of fennel and reserve. Pull off a few outer leaves and wash. Fill a large saucepan with enough water to cook the pasta. Add the fennel leaves and bring to the boil.

4 Heat the oil in a large frying pan and sauté the onion lightly until soft. Remove to a side dish. Add the sardines, a few at a time, and cook over a moderate heat until golden on both sides, turning once. When all the sardines have been cooked, gently return them to the pan. Add the onion, and the sultanas, pine nuts and fennel seeds. Season with salt and pepper.

5 Take about 60ml/4 tbsp of the boiling water for the pasta, and add it to the sauce. Add salt to the boiling water, and cook the pasta until *al dente*. Drain, and remove the fennel leaves. Dress the pasta with the sauce. Divide among four individual serving plates, arranging several sardines on each. Sprinkle with the reserved chopped fennel tops and serve at once.

Spaghetti with Olives and Capers

This spicy sauce originated in the Naples area. It can be quickly assembled using a few store-cupboard ingredients.

INGREDIENTS

Serves 4

60ml/4 tbsp olive oil
2 garlic cloves, finely chopped
small piece of dried red chilli, crumbled
50g/2oz can anchovy fillets, chopped
350g/12oz tomatoes, fresh or canned, chopped
115g/4oz/1 cup stoned black olives
30ml/2 tbsp capers, rinsed
15ml/1 tbsp tomato purée
400g/14oz spaghetti
30ml/2 tbsp chopped fresh parsley

1 Heat the oil in a large frying pan. Add the garlic and the dried red chilli, and cook for 2–3 minutes until the garlic is just golden.

2 Add the chopped anchovies, and mash them into the garlic with a fork.

3 Add the fresh or canned tomatoes, olives, capers and tomato purée. Stir well and cook over a moderate heat.

4 Cook the spaghetti in plenty of boiling salted water until *al dente*. Drain well.

5 Turn the spaghetti into the sauce. Increase the heat and cook for 3–4 minutes, turning the pasta constantly. Sprinkle with parsley and serve at once.

Linguine with Clam and Tomato Sauce

There are two types of traditional Italian clam sauce for pasta: one with tomatoes, as here, and another version without.

INGREDIENTS

Serves 4

900g/2lb fresh clams in the shell, or 350g/12oz bottled clams, with their liquid
90ml/6 tbsp olive oil
1 garlic clove, crushed
400g/14oz tomatoes, fresh or canned, very finely chopped
350g/12oz linguine
60ml/4 tbsp chopped fresh parsley
salt and ground black pepper

1 Scrub and rinse the clams well under cold running water. Place them in a large saucepan with a cupful of water, and heat until the clams begin to open. Lift each clam out as soon as it opens, and scoop it out of its shell using a small spoon. Place in a bowl.

2 If the clams are large, chop them into 2 or 3 pieces. Reserve any liquid from the shells in a separate bowl. When all the clams have opened (discard any that do not open), pour the cooking liquid into the juices from the clams, and strain them through a piece of kitchen paper to remove any sand. If using bottled clams, use the liquid from the jar.

3 Place the olive oil in a medium saucepan with the garlic. Cook over a moderate heat until golden.

4 Remove the garlic and discard. Add the chopped tomatoes to the oil, and pour in the clam liquid. Mix well and cook over a low to moderate heat until the sauce begins to dry out and thickens slightly.

5 Cook the pasta in plenty of boiling salted water until just *al dente*, following the instructions on the packet.

6 A minute or two before the pasta is cooked, stir the parsley and the clams into the tomato sauce, and increase the heat. Add pepper and taste for seasoning, adding salt if necessary. Drain the pasta and turn into a serving dish. Pour on the hot sauce and mix well before serving immediately.

Meals in Minutes

Spaghetti with Herb Sauce

Herbs make a wonderfully aromatic sauce – the heat from the pasta releases their flavours.

INGREDIENTS

Serves 4

50g/2oz chopped fresh mixed herbs, such as parsley, basil and thyme
2 garlic cloves, crushed
60ml/4 tbsp pine nuts, toasted
150ml/¼ pint/⅔ cup olive oil
350g/12oz dried spaghetti
60ml/4 tbsp freshly grated Parmesan cheese
salt and ground black pepper
basil leaves, to garnish

1 Put the herbs, garlic and half the pine nuts into a blender or food processor. With the machine running slowly, add the oil and process to form a thick purée.

2 Cook the spaghetti in plenty of boiling salted water for about 8 minutes until *al dente*. Drain.

3 Transfer the herb purée to a large warmed serving dish, then add the spaghetti and Parmesan. Toss well to coat the pasta with the sauce. Sprinkle over the remaining pine nuts and the basil leaves and serve immediately.

Beef Strips with Orange and Ginger

Stir-frying is one of the quickest ways to cook, but you do need to choose tender meat.

INGREDIENTS

Serves 4

450g/1lb lean beef rump, fillet or sirloin, cut into thin strips
finely grated rind and juice of 1 orange
15ml/1 tbsp light soy sauce
5ml/1 tsp cornflour
2.5cm/1in piece fresh root ginger, finely chopped
10ml/2 tsp sesame oil
1 large carrot, cut into thin strips
2 spring onions, thinly sliced
rice noodles, to serve

1 Place the beef strips in a bowl and sprinkle over the orange rind and juice. Leave to marinate for at least 30 minutes.

2 Drain the liquid from the meat and reserve, then mix the meat with the soy sauce, cornflour and fresh root ginger.

3 Heat the oil in a wok or large frying pan and add the beef. Stir-fry for 1 minute until lightly coloured, then add the carrot and stir-fry for a further 2–3 minutes.

4 Stir in the spring onions and reserved liquid, then cook, stirring, until boiling and thickened. Serve the beef hot with rice noodles.

Fettuccine with Ham and Cream

Prosciutto is perfect for this rich and delicious dish, which makes a very elegant starter.

INGREDIENTS

Serves 4

115g/4oz prosciutto crudo or other unsmoked ham (raw or cooked)
50g/2oz/¼ cup butter
2 shallots, very finely chopped
150ml/¼ pint/⅔ cup double cream
350g/12oz fettucine
50g/2oz/½ cup grated Parmesan cheese
salt and ground black pepper
fresh parsley sprig, to garnish

1 Cut the fat from the ham and chop both lean and fat parts separately into small squares.

2 Melt the butter in a medium frying pan and add the shallots and the squares of ham fat. Cook until golden. Add the lean ham, and cook for a further 2 minutes. Season with black pepper. Stir in the cream, and keep warm over a low heat while the pasta is cooking.

3 Cook the pasta in plenty of boiling salted water until *al dente*. Drain, turn into a warmed serving dish and toss with the sauce. Stir in the cheese and serve immediately, garnished with a sprig of parsley.

Tagliatelle with Smoked Salmon

In Italy smoked salmon is imported and quite expensive. This elegant creamy sauce makes a little go a long way. Use a mixture of green and white pasta if you wish.

INGREDIENTS

Serves 4–5

175g/6oz smoked salmon slices or ends, fresh or frozen
300ml/½ pint/1¼ cups single cream
pinch of ground mace or grated nutmeg
350g/12oz green and white tagliatelle
salt and ground black pepper
45ml/3 tbsp snipped fresh chives, to garnish

1 Cut the salmon into thin strips about 5cm/2in long. Place in a bowl with the cream and the mace or nutmeg. Stir, cover and allow to stand for at least 2 hours in a cool place (not in the fridge).

2 Cook the pasta in plenty of boiling salted water until it is just *al dente*.

3 Meanwhile, gently warm the cream and salmon mixture in a small saucepan, without boiling.

4 Drain the pasta, pour the sauce over and mix well. Season to taste and garnish with the chives.

Twin Cities Meatballs

Serve these meatballs without gravy as drinks party nibbles.

INGREDIENTS

Serves 6

30ml/2 tbsp butter or margarine
½ small onion, minced
350g/12oz/2¼ cups minced beef
115g/4oz/1 cup minced veal
225g/8oz/2 cups minced pork
1 egg
40g/1½oz/½ cup mashed potatoes
30ml/2 tbsp finely chopped fresh dill or parsley
1 garlic clove, crushed
5ml/1 tsp salt
2.5ml/½ tsp black pepper
2.5ml/½ tsp ground allspice
1.5ml/¼ tsp grated nutmeg
40g/1½oz/¾ cup fresh breadcrumbs
175ml/6fl oz/¾ cup milk
25g/1oz/¼ cup plain flour plus 15ml/1 tbsp extra
30ml/2 tbsp olive oil
175ml/6fl oz/¾ cup evaporated milk
buttered noodles, to serve

1 Melt the butter or margarine in a large frying pan. Add the onion and cook over a low heat until softened, about 8–10 minutes. Remove from the heat. Using a slotted spoon, transfer the onion to a large mixing bowl.

2 Add the beef, veal and pork, the egg, mashed potatoes, dill or parsley, garlic, salt, pepper, allspice and nutmeg to the bowl.

3 Put the breadcrumbs in a small bowl and add the milk. Stir until well moistened, then add to the other ingredients. Mix well.

4 Shape the mixture into balls about 2.5cm/1in in diameter. Roll them in 25g/1oz/¼ cup of the flour to coat all over.

5 Add the olive oil to the frying pan and heat over a medium heat. Add the meatballs and brown on all sides for 8–10 minutes. Shake the pan occasionally to roll the balls so they colour evenly. With a slotted spoon, remove the meatballs to a serving dish. Cover with foil and keep warm.

6 Stir the 15ml/1 tbsp of flour into the fat in the frying pan. Add the evaporated milk and mix in with a small whisk. Simmer for 3–4 minutes. Check the seasoning, and adjust if necessary.

7 Pour the gravy over the meatballs. Serve hot with buttered noodles.

Peasant Bolognese

A spicy version of a popular dish. Worcestershire sauce and chorizo sausages add an extra element to this perfect family standby.

INGREDIENTS

Serves 4

15ml/1 tbsp oil
225g/8oz/2 cups minced beef
1 onion, chopped
5ml/1 tsp chilli powder
15ml/1 tbsp Worcestershire sauce
25g/1oz/2 tbsp plain flour
150ml/¼ pint/⅔ cup beef stock
4 chorizo sausages
50g/2oz baby sweetcorn
200g/7oz can chopped tomatoes
15ml/1 tbsp chopped fresh basil
salt and ground black pepper
cooked spaghetti, to serve
fresh basil, to garnish

1 Heat the oil in a large pan and fry the minced beef for 5 minutes. Add the onion and chilli powder and cook for a further 3 minutes.

2 Stir in the Worcestershire sauce and flour. Cook for 1 minute before pouring in the stock.

3 Slice the chirozo sausages and halve the corn lengthways.

4 Stir in the sausages, tomatoes, sweetcorn and chopped basil. Season well and bring to the boil. Reduce the heat and simmer for 30 minutes. Serve with spaghetti, garnished with fresh basil.

COOK'S TIP

Make up the Bolognese sauce and freeze in conveniently sized portions for up to two months.

Tagliolini with Asparagus

Tagliolini are very thin egg noodles, more delicate in texture than spaghetti. They go well with this subtle cream sauce, flavoured with fresh asparagus.

INGREDIENTS

Serves 4

450g/1lb fresh asparagus
egg pasta sheets made with 2 eggs, or 350g/12oz fresh tagliolini or other egg noodles
50g/2oz/¼ cup butter
3 spring onions, finely chopped
3–4 fresh mint or basil leaves, finely chopped
150ml/¼ pint/⅔ cup double cream
50g/2oz/½ cup freshly grated Parmesan cheese
salt and ground black pepper

1 Peel the asparagus by inserting a small sharp knife at the base of the stalks and pulling upwards towards the tips. Drop them into a pan of boiling water and boil until just tender, about 4–6 minutes.

2 Remove from the pan, reserving the cooking water. Cut the tips off, and then cut the stalks into 4cm/1½in pieces. Set aside.

3 Make the egg pasta sheets, if using, and fold and cut into thin noodles, or feed through the narrowest setting of a pasta-making machine. Open them out and dry for 5–10 minutes.

4 Melt the butter in a large frying pan. Add the spring onions and herbs, and cook for 3–4 minutes. Stir in the cream and asparagus, and heat gently, but do not boil. Season to taste.

5 Bring the asparagus cooking water back to the boil. Add salt. Drop the noodles in all at once. Cook until just tender (freshly made noodles will cook in about 30–60 seconds). Drain thoroughly through a colander.

6 Turn the pasta into the pan with the sauce, increase the heat slightly and mix well. Stir in the Parmesan cheese. Mix well and serve at once.

Spicy Beef

If you are hungry and only have a few minutes to spare for cooking, this colourful and healthy dish is an excellent choice.

INGREDIENTS

Serves 4

15ml/1 tbsp oil
450g/1lb/4 cups minced beef
2.5cm/1in piece fresh root ginger, sliced
5ml/1 tsp Chinese five-spice powder
1 red chilli, sliced
50g/2oz mange-touts
1 red pepper, seeded and chopped
1 carrot, sliced
115g/4oz beansprouts
15ml/1 tbsp sesame oil
cooked Chinese egg noodles, to serve

1 Heat the oil in a wok until almost smoking. Add the minced beef and cook for about 3 minutes, stirring all the time.

2 Add the ginger, Chinese five-spice powder and chilli. Cook for 1 minute.

3 Add the mange-touts, the seeded and chopped red pepper and sliced carrot and cook for a further 3 minutes, stirring the mixture continuously.

4 Add the beansprouts and sesame oil and cook for a final 2 minutes. Serve immediately with Chinese egg noodles.

Stir-fried Sweet and Sour Chicken

There are few cookery concepts that are better suited to today's busy lifestyle than the all-in-one stir-fry. This one has a wonderful South-east Asian influence.

INGREDIENTS

Serves 4

275g/10oz Chinese egg noodles
30ml/2 tbsp vegetable oil
3 spring onions, chopped
1 garlic clove, crushed
2.5cm/1in piece fresh root ginger, peeled and grated
5ml/1 tsp hot paprika
5ml/1 tsp ground coriander
3 boneless chicken breasts, sliced
115g/4oz/1 cup sugar-snap peas, topped and tailed
115g/4oz baby sweetcorn, halved
225g/8oz fresh beansprouts
15ml/1 tbsp cornflour
45ml/3 tbsp soy sauce
45ml/3 tbsp lemon juice
15ml/1 tbsp sugar
45ml/3 tbsp chopped fresh coriander or spring onion tops, to garnish

1 Bring a large saucepan of salted water to the boil. Add the noodles and cook according to the instructions on the packet. Drain, cover and keep warm.

2 Heat the oil in a wok. Add the spring onions and cook over a gentle heat. Mix in the next five ingredients, then stir-fry for about 3–4 minutes. Add the next three ingredients and steam briefly. Add the noodles.

3 Combine the cornflour, soy sauce, lemon juice and sugar in a small bowl. Add to the wok and simmer briefly to thicken. Serve garnished with chopped coriander or spring onion tops.

Pasta Spirals with Pepperoni and Tomato

A warming supper dish, perfect for a cold winter's night. All types of sausage are suitable, but if using raw sausages, add them with the onion to cook thoroughly.

INGREDIENTS

Serves 4

1 onion
1 red pepper
1 green pepper
30ml/2 tbsp olive oil, plus extra for tossing the pasta
800g/1¾ lb canned chopped tomatoes
30ml/2 tbsp tomato purée
10ml/2 tsp paprika
175g/6oz pepperoni or chorizo sausage
45ml/3 tbsp chopped fresh parsley
450g/1lb pasta spirals, such as fusilli
salt and ground black pepper

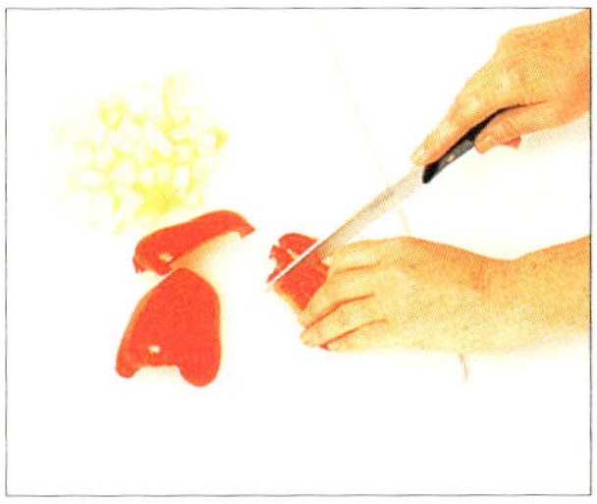

1 Chop the onion. Halve, core and seed the peppers. Cut the flesh into dice.

2 Heat the oil in a medium saucepan, add the onion and cook for 2–3 minutes until beginning to colour. Stir in the peppers, tomatoes, tomato purée and paprika, bring to the boil and simmer uncovered for about 15–20 minutes until reduced and thickened.

3 Slice the pepperoni or chorizo and stir into the sauce with 30ml/2 tbsp of the chopped parsley. Season to taste with salt and pepper.

4 While the sauce is simmering, cook the pasta in plenty of boiling salted water according to the instructions on the packet. Drain well. Toss the pasta with the remaining parsley in a little extra olive oil. Divide among four warmed bowls and top with sauce.

Farfalle with Prawns and Peas

A small amount of saffron in the sauce gives this dish a wonderful golden colour.

INGREDIENTS

Serves 4

- 45ml/3 tbsp olive oil
- 25g/1oz/2 tbsp butter
- 2 spring onions, chopped
- 350g/12oz/3 cups fresh or frozen peeled prawns
- 225g/8oz/1 cup frozen petit pois or peas, thawed
- 400g/14oz farfalle
- 250ml/8fl oz/1 cup dry white wine
- a few saffron strands or pinch of powdered saffron
- salt and ground black pepper
- 30ml/2 tbsp chopped fresh fennel or dill, to serve

1 Heat the oil and butter in a frying pan and sauté the spring onions lightly. Add the prawns and peas; cook for 2–3 minutes.

2 Cook the pasta in plenty of boiling salted water until just *al dente*.

3 Meanwhile, stir the wine and saffron into the prawn mixture.

4 Increase the heat and cook until the wine is reduced by about half. Add salt and pepper to taste. Cover and reduce the heat to low.

5 Drain the pasta and add it to the pan with the sauce. Stir over a high heat for 2–3 minutes, coating the pasta with the sauce. Sprinkle with the fresh herbs, and serve at once.

Short Pasta with Spring Vegetables

This colourful sauce makes the most of new crops of fresh, tender spring vegetables.

INGREDIENTS

Serves 6

- 1 or 2 small young carrots
- 2 spring onions
- 150g/5oz courgettes
- 2 tomatoes
- 75g/3oz/¾ cup shelled peas, fresh or frozen
- 75g/3oz fine green beans
- 1 yellow pepper
- 60ml/4 tbsp olive oil
- 25g/1oz/2 tbsp butter
- 1 garlic clove, finely chopped
- 5–6 fresh basil leaves, torn into pieces
- 500g/1¼lb short coloured or plain pasta, such as fusilli, penne or farfalle
- salt and ground black pepper
- freshly grated Parmesan cheese, to serve

1 Cut all the vegetables into small, bite-size pieces.

2 Heat the oil and butter in a large frying pan. Add the chopped vegetables, and cook over a moderate heat for 5–6 minutes, stirring occasionally. Add the garlic and the basil, and season with salt and pepper. Cover the pan and cook for a further 5–8 minutes, or until the vegetables are just tender.

3 Meanwhile, cook the pasta in plenty of boiling salted water until *al dente*. Before draining it, reserve a cupful of the pasta water.

4 Turn the pasta into the pan with the sauce, and mix well to distribute the vegetables. If the sauce seems too dry, add a few tablespoons of the reserved pasta water. Serve with the Parmesan handed round separately.

Tagliatelle with Prosciutto and Parmesan

This is a really simple dish, prepared in minutes from the best ingredients.

INGREDIENTS

Serves 4

115g/4oz prosciutto
450g/1lb tagliatelle
75g/3oz/6 tbsp butter
50g/2oz/½ cup freshly grated Parmesan cheese
salt and ground black pepper
a few fresh sage leaves, to garnish

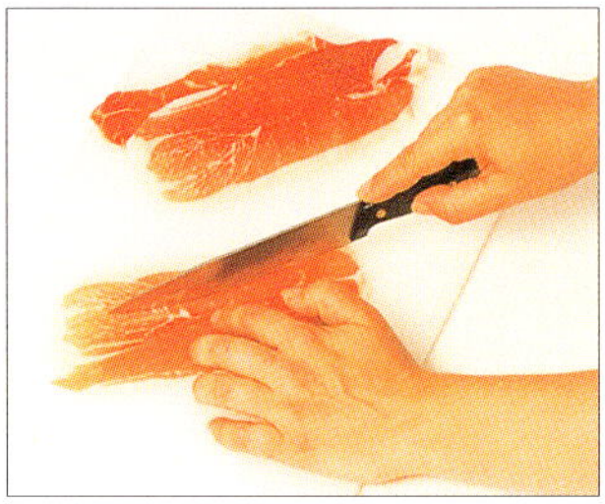

1 Cut the prosciutto into strips the same width as the tagliatelle. Cook the pasta in plenty of boiling salted water according to the instructions on the packet.

2 Meanwhile, melt the butter gently in a saucepan, stir in the prosciutto strips and heat through over a very gentle heat, being careful not to fry.

3 Drain the tagliatelle through a colander and pile into a warmed serving dish.

4 Sprinkle over all the Parmesan cheese and pour over the buttery prosciutto. Season well with black pepper and garnish with the sage leaves.

Capellini with Rocket and Mange-touts

A light but filling pasta dish with the added pepperiness of fresh rocket leaves.

INGREDIENTS

Serves 4

250g/9oz capellini or angel hair pasta
225g/8oz mange-touts
75g/3oz rocket leaves
50g/2oz/¼ cup pine nuts, roasted
30ml/2 tbsp finely grated Parmesan cheese (optional)
30ml/2 tbsp olive oil (optional)

1 Cook the capellini or angel-hair pasta in plenty of boiling salted water, according to the instructions on the packet, until just *al dente*.

2 Meanwhile, carefully top and tail the mange-touts, and discard any that are damaged.

3 As soon as the pasta is cooked, drop in the rocket and mange-touts. Drain immediately.

4 Toss the pasta with the roasted pine nuts, and Parmesan and olive oil if using. Serve at once.

Tagliatelle with Sun-dried Tomatoes

Choose plain sun-dried tomatoes for this sauce, instead of those preserved in oil, if you wish to reduce the fat content of the dish.

INGREDIENTS

Serves 4

1 garlic clove, crushed
1 celery stick, finely sliced
115g/4oz/1 cup sun-dried tomatoes, finely chopped
90ml/3½fl oz/scant ½ cup red wine
8 plum tomatoes
350g/12oz dried tagliatelle
salt and ground black pepper

1 Put the garlic, celery, sun-dried tomatoes and wine into a large saucepan. Gently cook for about 15 minutes.

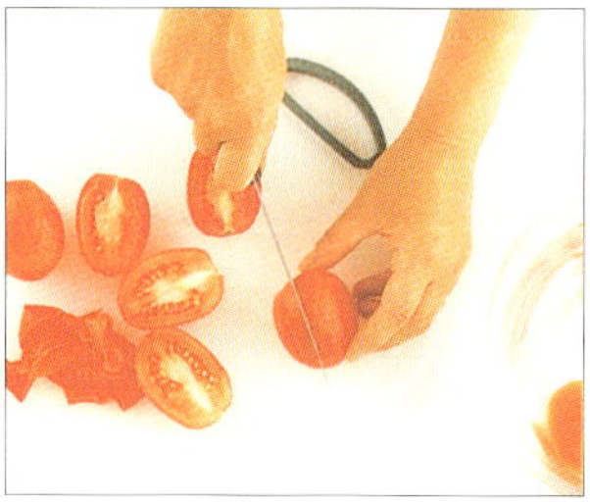

2 Slash the bottoms of the plum tomatoes and plunge into a saucepan of boiling water for 1 minute, then into a saucepan of cold water. Slip off their skins. Halve, remove the seeds and cores and roughly chop the flesh.

3 Add the plum tomatoes to the saucepan and simmer for a further 5 minutes. Season to taste.

4 Meanwhile, cook the tagliatelle in plenty of boiling salted water for 8–10 minutes, or until *al dente*. Drain well. Toss with half the sauce and serve on warmed plates, with the remaining sauce.

Pasta Rapido with Parsley Pesto

Here is a fresh and lively sauce that will appeal to even the most jaded of appetites.

INGREDIENTS

Serves 4

450g/1lb dried pasta, any shape
75g/3oz/¾ cup whole almonds
50g/2oz/½ cup flaked almonds
25g/1oz/¼ cup freshly grated Parmesan cheese
pinch of salt

For the sauce

40g/1½oz fresh parsley
2 garlic cloves, crushed
45ml/3 tbsp olive oil
45ml/3 tbsp lemon juice
5ml/1 tsp sugar
250ml/8fl oz/1 cup boiling water

1 Cook the pasta in plenty of boiling salted water, according to the instructions on the packet, until *al dente*. Toast the whole and flaked almonds separately under a moderate grill until golden brown. Set the flaked almonds aside.

2 For the sauce, chop the parsley finely in a blender or food processor. Add the whole almonds; reduce to a fine consistency. Add the garlic, oil, lemon juice, sugar and water. Combine to a sauce.

3 Drain the pasta and combine with half the sauce. (The remainder of the sauce will keep in a screw-top jar in the fridge for up to ten days.) Top with Parmesan and flaked almonds.

Pasta with Devilled Kidneys

Ask your butcher to prepare the kidneys for you if you prefer.

INGREDIENTS

Serves 4

8–10 lambs' kidneys
15ml/1 tbsp sunflower oil
25g/1oz/2 tbsp butter
10ml/2 tsp paprika
5–10ml/1–2 tsp mild grainy mustard
salt, to taste
chopped fresh parsley, to garnish
225g/8oz fresh pasta, to serve

1 Cut the kidneys in half and neatly cut out the white cores with scissors. Cut the kidneys again if very large.

2 Heat the oil and butter together. Add the kidneys and cook, turning frequently, for about 2 minutes. Blend the paprika and mustard together with a little salt and stir into the pan.

3 Continue cooking the kidneys, basting frequently, for about a further 3–4 minutes.

4 Cook the pasta for about 10–12 minutes, or according to the instructions on the packet. Serve the kidneys and their sauce, topped with the chopped fresh parsley, and accompanied by the pasta.

Golden-topped Pasta

When it comes to the children helping you to plan the menus, this is the sort of dish that always wins hands down. It is also perfect for "padding out" if you have to feed eight instead of four people.

INGREDIENTS

Serves 4–6

225g/8oz dried pasta shells or spirals
115g/4oz/⅔ cup chopped cooked ham, beef or turkey
350g/12oz par-cooked mixed vegetables, such as carrots, cauliflower, beans, etc
a little oil

For the cheese sauce

25g/1oz/2 tbsp butter
25g/1oz/2 tbsp plain flour
300ml/½ pint/1¼ cups milk
175g/6oz/1½ cups grated Cheddar cheese
5–10ml/1–2 tsp mustard
salt and ground black pepper

1 Cook the pasta according to the instructions on the packet. Drain and place in a flameproof dish with the chopped meat, the vegetables and 5–10ml/1–2 tsp oil.

2 Melt the butter in a saucepan, stir in the flour and cook for 1 minute, stirring. Remove from the heat and gradually stir in the milk. Return to the heat, bring to the boil, stirring and cook for 2 minutes. Add half the cheese, the mustard and seasoning to taste.

3 Spoon the sauce over the meat and vegetables. Sprinkle with the rest of the cheese and grill quickly until golden and bubbling.

Oriental Vegetable Noodles

You could use Chinese egg noodles instead of tagliarini if you prefer.

INGREDIENTS

Serves 6

500g/1¼lb thin tagliarini
1 red onion
115g/4oz shiitake mushrooms
45ml/3 tbsp sesame oil
45ml/3 tbsp dark soy sauce
15ml/1 tbsp balsamic vinegar
10ml/2 tsp caster sugar
5ml/1 tsp salt
celery leaves, to garnish

1 Cook the tagliarini in plenty of boiling salted water according to the instructions on the packet until *al dente*.

2 Thinly slice the red onion and the shiitake mushrooms, using a sharp knife.

3 Heat a wok, then add 15ml/1 tbsp of the sesame oil. When the oil is hot, stir-fry the onion and mushrooms for about 2 minutes.

4 Drain the tagliarini, then add to the wok with the soy sauce, balsamic vinegar, sugar and salt. Stir-fry for 1 minute, then add the remaining sesame oil, and serve garnished with celery leaves.

Stir-fried Vegetables with Pasta

This is a colourful Chinese-style dish, easily prepared using pasta instead of Chinese noodles.

INGREDIENTS

Serves 4

1 carrot
175g/6oz small courgettes
175g/6oz runner or other green beans
175g/6oz baby sweetcorn
450g/1lb ribbon pasta, such as tagliatelle
salt, to taste
30ml/2 tbsp corn oil, plus extra for tossing the pasta
1cm/½in piece fresh root ginger, peeled and finely chopped
2 garlic cloves, finely chopped
90ml/6 tbsp yellow bean sauce
6 spring onions, sliced into 2.5cm/1in lengths
30ml/2 tbsp dry sherry
5ml/1 tsp sesame seeds, to garnish

1 Slice the carrot and courgettes diagonally into chunks. Slice the beans diagonally. Cut the baby sweetcorn diagonally in half.

2 Cook the pasta in plenty of boiling salted water according to the instructions on the packet. Drain, then rinse under hot water. Toss in a little corn oil.

3 Heat 30ml/2 tbsp oil until smoking in a wok or frying pan and add the ginger and garlic. Stir-fry for 30 seconds, then add the carrots, beans and courgettes.

4 Stir-fry for 3–4 minutes, then stir in the yellow bean sauce. Stir-fry for 2 minutes, add the spring onions, sherry and pasta and stir-fry for 1 minute or until piping hot. Sprinkle with sesame seeds and serve immediately.

Lasagne Rolls

Perhaps a more elegant presentation than ordinary lasagne, but just as tasty and popular. You will need to boil "no-need-to-cook" lasagne as it needs to be soft enough to roll!

INGREDIENTS

Serves 4

8-10 lasagne sheets
225g/8oz fresh leaf spinach, well washed
115g/4oz mushrooms, sliced
115g/4oz mozzarella cheese, thinly sliced
Lentil Bolognese (see below)

Béchamel Sauce

50g/2oz/scant ½ cup all-purpose flour
45ml/3 tbsp butter or margarine
600ml/1 pint/2½ cups milk
bay leaf
salt and ground black pepper
freshly grated nutmeg
freshly grated Parmesan or pecorino cheese, to serve

1 Cook the lasagne sheets according to instructions on the package, or until *al dente*. Drain and allow to cool.

2 Cook the spinach in the tiniest amount of water for 2 minutes then add the sliced mushrooms and cook for a further 2 minutes. Drain very well, pressing out all the excess liquor, and chop the spinach roughly.

3 Put all the béchamel ingredients into a saucepan and bring slowly to a boil, stirring until the sauce is thick and smooth. Simmer for 2 minutes with the bay leaf, then season well and stir in the grated nutmeg to taste.

4 Lay out the pasta sheets and spread with the béchamel sauce, spinach, mushrooms and mozzarella. Roll up each one and place in a large shallow casserole dish with the join face down in the dish.

5 Remove and discard the bay leaf and then pour the sauce over the pasta. Sprinkle the cheese and place under a hot grill to brown.

VARIATION

Needless to say, the fillings in this recipe could be any of your own choice. Another favourite is a lightly stir-fried mixture of colourful vegetables such as peppers, courgettes, aubergines and mushrooms, topped with a cheese béchamel as above, or with a fresh tomato sauce, which is especially good in summer.

Lentil Bolognese

A really useful sauce to serve with pasta, such as Lasagne Rolls (as above), as a crêpe stuffing or even as a protein-packed sauce for vegetables.

INGREDIENTS

Serves 6

1 onion
2 garlic cloves, crushed
2 carrots, coarsely grated
2 celery stalks, chopped
45ml/3 tbsp olive oil
150g/5oz/⅔ cup red lentils
14 oz can chopped tomatoes
45ml/3 tbsp tomato paste
475ml/16fl oz/2 cups stock
15ml/1 tbsp fresh marjoram, chopped, or 5ml/1 tsp dried marjoram
salt and ground black pepper

1 In a large saucepan, gently fry the onion, garlic, carrots and celery in the oil for about 5 minutes, until they are soft.

2 Add the lentils, tomatoes, tomato paste, stock and marjoram, and season to taste.

3 Bring the mixture to a boil, then partially cover with a lid and simmer for 20 minutes until thick and soft. Use the bolognese sauce as required.

Tagliatelle with Parma Ham and Asparagus

A stunning sauce, this is worth every effort to serve at a dinner party.

INGREDIENTS

Serves 4

350g/12oz tagliatelle
25g/1oz/2 tbsp butter
15ml/1 tbsp olive oil
225g/8oz asparagus tips
1 garlic clove, chopped
115g/4oz Parma ham, sliced into strips
30ml/2 tbsp chopped fresh sage
150ml/¼ pint/⅔ cup single cream
115g/4oz/1 cup grated chive-and-onion double Gloucester cheese
115g/4oz/1 cup grated Gruyère cheese
salt and ground black pepper
fresh sage sprigs, to garnish

1 Cook the pasta in plenty of boiling salted water according to the instructions on the packet.

2 Melt the butter and oil in a frying pan and gently fry the asparagus tips for about 5 minutes, stirring occasionally, until they are almost tender.

3 Stir in the garlic and Parma ham and fry for 1 minute.

4 Stir in the chopped sage and fry for a further 1 minute.

5 Pour in the cream and bring the mixture to the boil.

6 Add the cheeses and simmer gently, stirring occasionally, until thoroughly melted. Season.

7 Drain the pasta thoroughly and toss with the sauce to coat. Serve immediately, garnished with fresh sage sprigs.

Curly Spaghetti with Walnut and Cream

A classic Italian dish with a strong, nutty flavour, this should be served with a delicately flavoured salad.

INGREDIENTS

Serves 4

350g/12oz curly spaghetti (fusilli col buco)
50g/2oz/½ cup walnut pieces
25g/1oz/2 tbsp butter
300ml/½ pint/1¼ cups milk
50g/2oz/1 cup fresh breadcrumbs
25g/1oz/2 tbsp freshly grated Parmesan cheese
pinch of freshly grated nutmeg
salt and ground black pepper
fresh rosemary sprigs, to garnish

1 Cook the pasta in plenty of boiling salted water according to the instructions on the packet. Meanwhile, preheat the grill.

2 Spread the walnuts evenly over the grill pan. Grill for about 5 minutes, turning occasionally until evenly toasted.

3 Remove the walnuts from the heat, place in a clean dish towel and rub away the skins. Roughly chop the nuts.

4 Heat the butter and milk in a saucepan until the butter is completely melted.

5 Stir in the breadcrumbs and nuts and heat gently for 2 minutes, stirring constantly until thickened.

6 Add the Parmesan cheese, nutmeg and seasoning to taste.

7 Drain the pasta thoroughly through a colander and toss in the sauce. Serve immediately, garnished with fresh sprigs of rosemary.

Cannelloni al Forno

A lighter alternative to the usual beef-filled, béchamel-coated version. Fill with ricotta cheese, onion and mushroom for a vegetarian version.

INGREDIENTS

Serves 4–6

450g/1lb skinless, boneless chicken breast, cooked
225g/8oz mushrooms
2 garlic cloves, crushed
30ml/2 tbsp chopped fresh parsley
15ml/1 tbsp chopped fresh tarragon
1 egg, beaten
freshly squeezed lemon juice
12–18 cannelloni tubes
1 quantity Napoletana Sauce
50g/2oz/½ cup freshly grated Parmesan cheese
salt and ground black pepper
fresh parsley sprig, to garnish

1 Preheat the oven to 200°C/400°F/Gas 6. Place the chicken in a blender or food processor and process until finely minced. Transfer to a bowl.

2 Place the mushrooms, garlic, parsley and tarragon in the blender or food processor and process until finely minced.

3 Beat the mushroom mixture into the chicken with the egg, salt and ground black pepper and lemon juice to taste.

4 If necessary, cook the cannelloni in plenty of salted boiling water according to the instructions on the packet. Drain well and pat dry on a clean dish towel.

5 Place the filling in a piping bag fitted with a large plain nozzle. Use to fill each tube of cannelloni.

6 Lay the filled cannelloni tightly together in a single layer in a buttered shallow ovenproof dish. Spoon over the tomato sauce and sprinkle with Parmesan cheese. Bake in the oven for 30 minutes or until brown and bubbling. Serve the cannelloni garnished with a sprig of parsley.

Magnificent Marrow

At autumn time, marrows – with their wonderful green and cream stripes – look so attractive and tempting. They make delicious, inexpensive main courses, just right for a satisfying family meal.

INGREDIENTS

Serves 4–6

250g/9oz pasta shells
1.5–1.75kg/3–4½lb marrow
1 onion, chopped
1 pepper, seeded and chopped
15ml/1 tbsp fresh root ginger, grated
2 garlic cloves, crushed
45ml/3 tbsp sunflower oil
4 large tomatoes, skinned and chopped
50g/2oz/½ cup pine nuts
15ml/1 tbsp chopped fresh basil
salt and ground black pepper
grated cheese, to serve (optional)

1 Preheat the oven to 190°C/375°F/Gas 5. Cook the pasta in plenty of boiling salted water according to the instructions on the packet, slightly overcooking it so it is just a little soft. Drain well and reserve.

2 Cut the marrow in half lengthways and scoop out and discard the seeds. Use a small sharp knife and tablespoon to scoop out the marrow flesh. Chop the flesh roughly.

3 Gently fry the onion, pepper, ginger and garlic in the oil for 5 minutes then add the marrow flesh, tomatoes and seasoning. Cover and cook for 10–12 minutes until the vegetables are soft.

4 Add the pasta, pine nuts and basil to the pan, stir well and set aside until required.

5 Meanwhile, place the marrow halves in a roasting tin, season lightly and pour a little water around the marrow, taking care it does not spill inside. Cover with foil and bake for 15 minutes.

6 Remove the foil, discard the water and fill the shells with the vegetable mixture. Cover with foil and return to the oven for a further 20–25 minutes.

7 Top with cheese, if using. To serve, scoop out of the "shell" or cut into sections.

Tagliatelle with Chicken and Herb Sauce

Serve this delicious dish with its wine-flavoured sauce and a fresh green salad.

INGREDIENTS

Serves 4

30ml/2 tbsp olive oil
1 red onion, cut into wedges
350g/12oz tagliatelle
1 garlic clove, chopped
350g/12oz chicken, diced
300ml/½ pint/1¼ cups dry vermouth
45ml/3 tbsp chopped fresh mixed herbs
150ml/¼ pint/⅔ cup fromage frais
salt and ground black pepper
shredded fresh mint, to garnish

1 Heat the oil in a large frying pan and fry the red onion for 10 minutes until softened and the layers have separated.

2 Cook the pasta in plenty of boiling salted water according to the instructions on the packet.

3 Add the garlic and chicken to the frying pan and fry for 10 minutes, stirring occasionally, until the chicken is browned all over and cooked through.

4 Pour in the vermouth, bring to boiling point and boil rapidly until reduced by about half.

5 Stir in the herbs, fromage frais and seasoning and heat through gently, but do not boil.

6 Drain the pasta thoroughly and toss with the sauce to coat. Serve immediately, garnished with shredded fresh mint.

Penne with Sausage and Parmesan Sauce

Spicy sausage tossed in a cheesy tomato sauce is delicious served on a bed of cooked pasta.

INGREDIENTS

Serves 4

350g/12oz penne
450g/1lb ripe tomatoes
30ml/2 tbsp olive oil
225g/8oz chorizo sausage, diagonally sliced
1 garlic clove, chopped
30ml/2 tbsp chopped fresh flat leaf parsley
grated rind of 1 lemon
50g/2oz/½ cup freshly grated Parmesan cheese
salt and ground black pepper
finely chopped fresh flat leaf parsley, to garnish

1 Cook the pasta in plenty of boiling salted water according to the instructions on the packet.

2 Slash the bottoms of the tomatoes with a knife, making a cross. Place in a large bowl, cover with boiling water and leave to stand for 45 seconds. Plunge into cold water for 30 seconds, then peel off the skins and roughly chop the flesh.

3 Heat the oil in a frying pan and fry the sliced chorizo sausage for 5 minutes, stirring from time to time, until browned.

4 Add the chopped tomatoes, garlic, parsley and grated lemon rind. Heat through gently, stirring, for 1 minute.

5 Add the grated Parmesan cheese and season to taste.

6 Drain the pasta well through a colander and toss it with the sauce to coat. Serve immediately, garnished with finely chopped fresh flat leaf parsley.

Short Pasta with Cauliflower

This is a pasta version of cauliflower cheese. The cauliflower water is used to cook the pasta.

INGREDIENTS

Serves 6

1 cauliflower
475ml/16fl oz/2 cups milk
1 bay leaf
50g/2oz/¼ cup butter
50g/2oz/½ cup flour
75g/3oz/¾ cup freshly grated Parmesan or Cheddar cheese
500g/1¼lb pennoni rigati or other short pasta
salt and ground black pepper

1 Bring a large pan of water to the boil. Wash the cauliflower well, and separate it into florets. Boil the florets until they are just tender, about 8–10 minutes. Remove from the pan with a slotted spoon. Chop the cauliflower into bite-size pieces and set aside. Do not discard the cooking water in the pan.

2 Make a béchamel sauce by gently heating the milk with the bay leaf in a small saucepan. Do not let it boil. Melt the butter in a medium heavy-based saucepan. Add the flour, and mix in well with a wire whisk ensuring there are no lumps. Cook for 2–3 minutes, but do not let the butter burn.

3 Strain the hot milk into the flour and butter mixture all at once, and mix smoothly with the wire whisk.

4 Bring the sauce to the boil, stirring constantly, and cook for a further 4-5 minutes. Season to taste. Add the cheese, and stir over a low heat until melted. Stir in the cauliflower. Keep warm.

5 Bring the cauliflower cooking water back to the boil. Add salt, stir in the pasta and cook until *al dente*. Drain, and tip the pasta into a warmed serving dish. Pour over the sauce. Mix well, and serve at once.

Spaghetti with Bacon and Onion

This easy sauce is quickly made from ingredients that are almost always at hand.

INGREDIENTS

Serves 6

30ml/2 tbsp olive oil or lard
115g/4oz unsmoked streaky bacon, cut into matchsticks
1 small onion, finely chopped
120ml/4fl oz/½ cup dry white wine
450g/1lb tomatoes, fresh or canned, chopped
1.5ml/¼ tsp thyme leaves
600g/1lb 6oz spaghetti
salt and ground black pepper
freshly grated Parmesan cheese, to serve

1 In a medium frying pan, heat the oil or lard. Add the bacon and onion, and cook over a low to moderate heat until the onion is golden and the bacon has rendered its fat and is beginning to brown, about 8–10 minutes.

2 Add the wine to the bacon and onion, increase the heat and cook rapidly until the liquid boils off. Add the tomatoes, thyme, salt and pepper. Cover and cook over a moderate heat for 10–15 minutes.

3 Cook the pasta in plenty of boiling salted water until *al dente*. Drain, toss with the sauce and hand round the grated Parmesan cheese separately.

Pasta Bows with Fennel and Walnut

A scrumptious blend of walnuts and crisp steamed fennel.

INGREDIENTS

Serves 4

75g/3oz/½ cup walnuts, roughly chopped
1 garlic clove, chopped
25g/1oz fresh flat-leaf parsley, picked from the stalks
115g/4oz/½ cup ricotta cheese
450g/1lb pasta bows
450g/1lb fennel bulbs
chopped walnuts, to garnish

1 Place the chopped walnuts, garlic and parsley in a food processor. Pulse until roughly chopped. Transfer to a bowl and stir in the ricotta cheese.

2 Cook the pasta following the instructions on the packet until *al dente*. Drain thoroughly.

3 Slice the fennel thinly and steam for 4–5 minutes until just tender but still crisp.

4 Return the pasta to the pan and add the walnut mixture and the fennel. Toss well and sprinkle with the chopped walnuts to garnish. Serve immediately.

Pasta Tossed with Grilled Vegetables

A hearty dish to be eaten with crusty bread and washed down with a robust red wine. Try barbecuing the vegetables for a really smoky flavour.

INGREDIENTS

Serves 4

1 aubergine
2 courgettes
1 red pepper
3 garlic cloves, unpeeled
about 150ml/¼ pint/⅔ cup good olive oil
450g/1lb ribbon pasta pappardelle
salt and ground black pepper
a few sprigs fresh thyme, to garnish

1 Preheat the grill. With a sharp knife, slice the aubergine and courgettes lengthways.

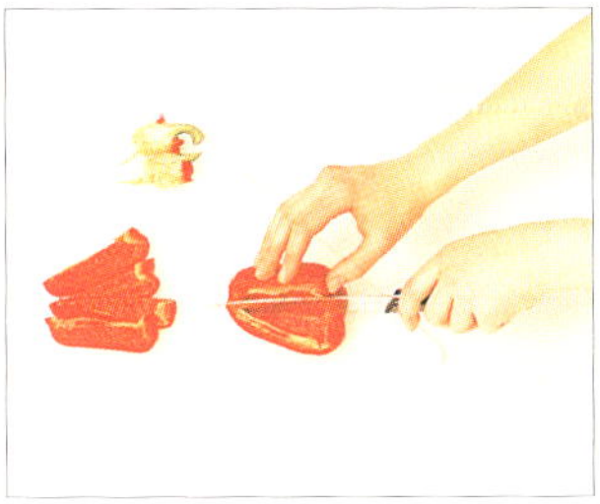

2 Halve the pepper, cut out the stalk and white pith and scrape out the seeds. Slice the pepper lengthways into eight pieces.

3 Line a grill pan with foil and arrange the vegetables and unpeeled garlic in a single layer over the foil. Brush liberally with oil and season with salt and ground black pepper.

4 Grill until slightly charred, turning once. If necessary, cook the vegetables in two batches.

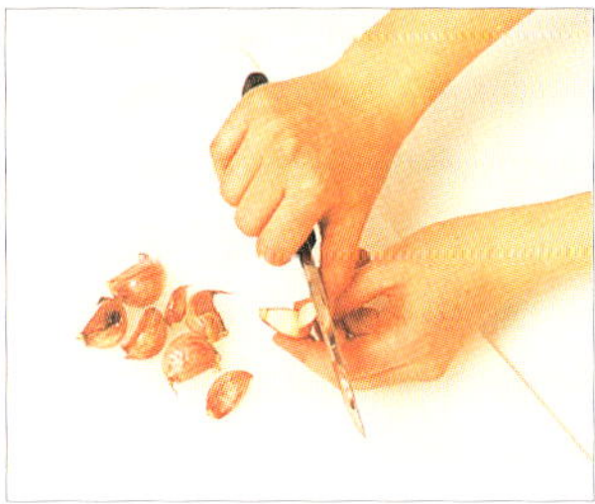

5 Cool the garlic, remove the charred skins and halve. Toss the vegetables with olive oil and keep warm.

6 Meanwhile cook the pasta in plenty of boiling salted water according to the instructions on the packet. Drain well and toss with the grilled vegetables. Serve immediately garnished with sprigs of fresh thyme.

Spinach and Ricotta Conchiglie

Large pasta shells are designed to hold a variety of delicious stuffings. Few are more pleasing than this mixture of spinach and ricotta.

INGREDIENTS

Serves 4

350g/12oz large conchiglie
450ml/¾ pint/1¾ cups passata or tomato pulp
275g/10oz frozen chopped spinach, thawed
50g/2oz crustless white bread, crumbled
120ml/4fl oz/½ cup milk
45ml/3 tbsp olive oil
250g/9oz ricotta cheese
pinch of grated nutmeg
1 garlic clove, crushed
15ml/1 tsbp olive oil
2.5ml/½ tsp black olive paste (optional)
25g/1oz/2 tbsp pine nuts
Parmesan cheese, for sprinkling
salt and ground black pepper

1 Cook the pasta in plenty of boiling salted water according to the instructions on the packet. Rinse under cold water, drain and reserve until needed.

2 Pour the passata or tomato pulp into a nylon sieve over a bowl and strain to thicken. Place the spinach in another sieve and press out any excess liquid with the back of a spoon.

3 Place the bread, milk and oil in a blender or food processor and process to combine. Add the spinach and ricotta cheese and season with salt, pepper and grated nutmeg.

4 Combine the passata or tomato pulp with the garlic, olive oil and olive paste, if using. Spread the sauce evenly over the base of an ovenproof dish.

5 Spoon the spinach mixture into a piping bag fitted with a large plain nozzle and fill the pasta shapes (alternatively fill with a spoon). Arrange the pasta shapes over the sauce.

6 Preheat the grill to a moderate heat. Heat the pasta through in the microwave on a high power for 4 minutes. Scatter with Parmesan cheese and pine nuts, and finish under the grill to brown the cheese until bubbling.

SALADS & STARTERS

Wholemeal Pasta Salad

This substantial vegetarian salad is easily assembled from any combination of seasonal vegetables. Use raw or lightly blanched vegetables, or a mixture of both.

INGREDIENTS

Serves 8

450g/1lb short wholemeal pasta, such as fusilli or penne
45ml/3 tbsp olive oil
2 carrots
1 small bunch broccoli
175g/6oz/1½ cups shelled peas, fresh or frozen
1 red or yellow pepper
2 celery sticks
4 spring onions
1 large tomato
75g/3oz/¾ cup stoned olives
115g/4oz/1 cup diced Cheddar or mozzarella cheese or a combination of both
salt and ground black pepper

For the dressing

45ml/3 tbsp white wine or balsamic vinegar
60ml/4 tbsp olive oil
15ml/1 tbsp Dijon mustard
15ml/1 tbsp sesame seeds
10ml/2 tsp chopped mixed fresh herbs, such as parsley, thyme and basil

1 Cook the pasta in plenty of boiling salted water until *al dente*. Drain, and rinse under cold water to stop the cooking. Drain well and turn into a large bowl. Toss with 45ml/3 tbsp of the olive oil and set aside. Allow the pasta to cool completely.

2 Lightly blanch the carrots, broccoli and peas in a large pan of boiling water. Refresh under cold water. Drain well.

3 Chop the carrots and broccoli into bite-size pieces and add to the pasta with the peas. Slice the pepper, celery, spring onions and tomato into small pieces. Add them to the salad with the olives.

4 Make the dressing in a small bowl by combining the vinegar with the oil and mustard. Stir in the sesame seeds and herbs. Mix the dressing into the salad. Taste for seasoning, adding salt, pepper or more olive oil and vinegar if necessary. Stir in the cheese, then allow the salad to stand for about 15 minutes before serving.

Pasta Salad with Olives

This delicious salad combines all the flavours of the Mediterranean. It is an excellent way of serving pasta and is particularly suitable for a hot summer's day.

INGREDIENTS

Serves 6

450g/1lb short pasta, such as medium shells, farfalle or penne
60ml/4 tbsp extra virgin olive oil
10 sun-dried tomatoes, thinly sliced
30ml/2 tbsp capers, in brine or salted
115g/4oz/1 cup stoned black olives
2 garlic cloves, finely chopped
45ml/3 tbsp balsamic vinegar
45ml/3 tbsp chopped fresh parsley
salt and ground black pepper

1 Cook the pasta in plenty of boiling salted water until *al dente*. Drain and rinse under cold water to stop the cooking. Drain well and turn into a large bowl. Toss with the olive oil and set aside until required.

2 Soak the tomatoes in a bowl of hot water for 10 minutes. Do not discard the water. Rinse the capers well. If they have been preserved in salt, soak them in a little hot water for 10 minutes. Rinse again.

3 Combine the olives, tomatoes, capers, garlic and vinegar in a small bowl. Season with salt and ground black pepper.

4 Stir the olive mixture into the cooked pasta and toss well. Add 30–45ml/2–3 tbsp of the tomato soaking water if the salad seems too dry. Toss with the parsley and allow to stand for 15 minutes before serving.

Artichoke Pasta Salad

Broccoli and black olives add colour to this delicious salad.

INGREDIENTS

Serves 4

105ml/7 tbsp olive oil
1 red pepper, quartered, seeded, and thinly sliced
1 onion, halved and thinly sliced
5ml/1 tsp dried thyme
45ml/3 tbsp sherry vinegar
450g/1lb pasta shapes, such as penne or fusilli
2 x 175g/6oz jars marinated artichoke hearts, drained and thinly sliced
150g/5oz cooked broccoli, chopped
20–25 salt-cured black olives, stoned and chopped
30ml/2 tbsp chopped fresh parsley
salt and ground black pepper

1 Heat 30ml/2 tbsp of the olive oil in a non-stick frying pan. Add the red pepper and onion and cook over a low heat until just soft, about 8–10 minutes, stirring from time to time.

2 Stir in the thyme, 1.5ml/¼ tsp salt and the vinegar. Cook, stirring, for a further 30 seconds, then set aside.

3 Cook the pasta in plenty of boiling salted water according to the instructions on the packet until *al dente*. Drain, rinse with hot water, then drain again. Transfer to a large bowl. Add 30ml/2 tbsp of the oil and toss well to coat thoroughly.

4 Add the artichokes, broccoli, olives, parsley, onion mixture and remaining oil to the pasta. Season with salt and pepper. Stir to blend. Leave to stand for at least 1 hour before serving or chill overnight. Serve the salad at room temperature.

Smoked Trout Pasta Salad

Bulb fennel gives this salad a lovely aniseed flavour.

INGREDIENTS

Serves 6

15ml/1 tbsp butter
115g/4oz minced bulb fennel
6 spring onions, 2 minced and 4 thinly sliced
225g/8oz skinless smoked trout fillets, flaked
45ml/3 tbsp chopped fresh dill
115g/4oz/½ cup mayonnaise
10ml/2 tsp fresh lemon juice
30ml/2 tbsp whipping cream
450g/1lb small pasta shapes, such as shells
salt and ground black pepper
fresh dill sprigs, to garnish

1 Melt the butter in a small non-stick frying pan. Add the fennel and minced spring onions and season lightly with salt and black pepper. Cook over a medium heat for 3–5 minutes, or until just softened. Transfer to a large bowl and leave to cool slightly.

2 Add the sliced spring onions, trout, dill, mayonnaise, lemon juice and cream. Mix gently until well blended.

3 Cook the pasta in plenty of boiling salted water according to the instructions on the packet until *al dente*. Drain thoroughly and leave to cool.

4 Add the pasta to the vegetable and trout mixture and toss to coat evenly. Taste for seasoning and adjust if necessary. Serve the salad lightly chilled or at room temperature, garnished with dill.

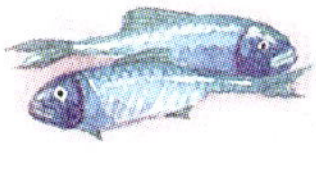

Tuna Pasta Salad

This easy pasta salad uses canned beans and tuna for a quick main course dish.

INGREDIENTS

Serves 6–8

450g/1lb short pasta, such as macaroni or farfalle
60ml/4 tbsp olive oil
2 x 200g/7oz cans tuna, drained and flaked
2 x 400g/14oz cans cannellini or borlotti beans, rinsed and drained
1 small red onion
2 celery sticks
juice of 1 lemon
30ml/2 tbsp chopped fresh parsley
salt and ground black pepper

1 Cook the pasta in plenty of boiling salted water until *al dente*. Drain, and rinse under cold water to stop the cooking. Drain well and turn into a large bowl. Toss with the olive oil and set aside. Allow to cool completely.

2 Mix the flaked tuna and the beans into the cooked pasta. Slice the onion and celery very thinly and add them to the pasta.

3 Combine the lemon juice with the parsley. Mix into the other ingredients. Season with salt and pepper. Allow the salad to stand for at least 1 hour before serving.

Chicken Pasta Salad

This salad uses leftover chicken from a roast or a cold poached chicken breast if you prefer.

INGREDIENTS

Serves 4

350g/12oz short pasta, such as mezze, rigatoni, fusilli or penne
45ml/3 tbsp olive oil
225g/8oz cold cooked chicken
2 small red and yellow peppers
50g/2oz/½ cup stoned green olives
4 spring onions, chopped
45ml/3 tbsp mayonnaise
5ml/1 tsp Worcestershire sauce
15ml/1 tbsp white wine vinegar
salt and ground black pepper
a few fresh basil leaves, to garnish

1 Cook the pasta in plenty of boiling salted water until *al dente*. Drain, and rinse under cold water to stop the cooking. Drain well and turn into a large bowl. Toss with the olive oil and set aside. Allow to cool completely.

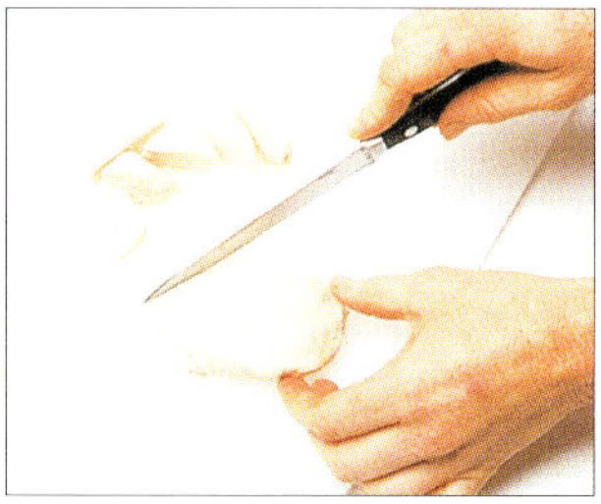

2 Cut the chicken into bite-size pieces, removing any bones. Cut the peppers into small pieces.

3 Combine all the ingredients except the pasta in a medium bowl. Taste for seasoning, then mix into the pasta. Serve well chilled, garnished with basil leaves.

Pasta, Asparagus and Potato Salad

A meal in itself, this is a real treat when made with fresh asparagus just in season.

INGREDIENTS

Serves 4

225g/8oz wholemeal pasta shapes
60ml/4 tbsp extra virgin olive oil
350g/12oz baby new potatoes
225g/8oz fresh asparagus
115g/4oz Parmesan cheese
salt and ground black pepper

1 Cook the pasta in boiling salted water according to the instructions on the packet. Drain well and toss with the olive oil and salt and pepper while still warm.

2 Wash the potatoes and cook in boiling salted water for about 12–15 minutes or until tender. Drain and toss with the pasta.

3 Trim any woody ends off the asparagus and halve the stalks if very long. Blanch in boiling salted water for 6 minutes until bright green and still crunchy. Drain, refresh in cold water and allow to cool. Drain and pat dry.

4 Toss the asparagus with the potatoes and pasta, season and transfer to a shallow bowl. Using a rotary vegetable peeler, shave over the Parmesan. Serve immediately.

Roquefort and Walnut Pasta Salad

This is a simple earthy salad, relying totally on the quality of the ingredients. There is no real substitute for Roquefort – a blue-veined ewe's-milk cheese which comes from south-western France.

INGREDIENTS

Serves 4

225g/8oz pasta shapes
mixed salad leaves, such as rocket, curly endive, lamb's lettuce, baby spinach, radicchio, etc
30ml/2 tbsp walnut oil
60ml/4 tbsp sunflower oil
30ml/2 tbsp red wine vinegar or sherry vinegar
225g/8oz Roquefort cheese, roughly crumbled
115g/4oz/1 cup walnut halves
salt and ground black pepper

1 Cook the pasta in plenty of boiling salted water according to the instructions on the packet. Drain well and cool. Wash and dry the salad leaves and place them in a large bowl.

2 Whisk together the walnut oil, sunflower oil, vinegar and salt and pepper to taste.

3 Pile the pasta in the centre of the leaves, scatter over the crumbled Roquefort and pour over the dressing.

4 Scatter over the walnuts. Toss just before serving.

COOK'S TIP

Try toasting the walnuts under the grill for a couple of minutes to release the flavour.

Pasta and Beetroot Salad

Colour is vital at a party table, and this salad is certainly eye-catching. Prepare the egg and avocado at the last moment to avoid discoloration.

INGREDIENTS

Serves 8

2 uncooked beetroots, scrubbed
225g/8oz pasta shells or twists
45ml/3 tbsp vinaigrette dressing
2 celery sticks, thinly sliced
3 spring onions, sliced
75g/3oz/¾ cup walnuts or hazelnuts, roughly chopped
1 eating apple, cored, halved and sliced
salt and ground black pepper

For the dressing

60ml/4 tbsp mayonnaise
45ml/3 tbsp natural yogurt or fromage frais
30ml/2 tbsp milk
10ml/2 tsp creamed horseradish

To serve

curly lettuce leaves
3 eggs, hard-boiled and chopped
2 ripe avocados
1 box salad cress

1 Boil the beetroots, without peeling, in lightly salted water until they are just tender, about 1 hour. Drain, cool, then peel and chop. Set aside.

2 Cook the pasta in plenty of boiled salted water according to the instructions on the packet. Drain, toss in the vinaigrette and season well. Leave to cool then mix with the beetroot, celery, onions, nuts and apple in a bowl.

3 Stir all the dressing ingredients together and then mix into the pasta. Chill well.

4 To serve, line a salad bowl with the lettuce and spoon in the salad. Scatter over the chopped egg. Peel and slice the avocados and arrange them on top then sprinkle over the cress.

Warm Pasta Salad with Ham and Egg

In the summer months when the weather is hot, try serving your pasta calda, *as a warm salad. Here it is served with ham, eggs and asparagus. A mustard dressing made from the thick part of asparagus provides a rich accompaniment.*

INGREDIENTS

Serves 4

450g/1lb asparagus
salt, to taste
450g/1lb dried tagliatelle
225g/8oz sliced cooked ham, 5mm/¼in thick, cut into fingers
2 eggs, hard-boiled and sliced
50g/2oz Parmesan cheese, shaved

For the dressing

50g/2oz cooked potato
75g/5 tbsp olive oil, preferably Sicilian
15ml/1 tbsp lemon juice
10ml/2 tsp Dijon mustard
120ml/4fl oz/½ cup vegetable stock

1 Bring a saucepan of salted water to the boil. Trim and discard the tough woody parts of the asparagus. Cut the asparagus in half and boil the thicker halves for 12 minutes. After 6 minutes throw in the tips. Refresh under cold water until warm, then drain.

2 Finely chop 150g/5oz of the asparagus middle section. Place in a blender or food processor with the dressing ingredients and process until smooth. Season to taste with salt and pepper.

3 Cook the pasta in plenty of boiling salted water according to the instructions on the packet. Refresh under cold water until warm, then drain. Dress with the asparagus sauce and turn out on to four pasta plates. Top the pasta with the ham, hard-boiled eggs and asparagus tips. Finish with Parmesan cheese shavings.

Avocado, Tomato and Mozzarella Salad

This salad is made from ingredients representing the colours of the Italian flag – a sunny cheerful dish!

INGREDIENTS

Serves 4

175g/6oz farfalle
6 ripe red tomatoes
225g/8oz mozzarella cheese
1 large ripe avocado
30ml/2 tbsp chopped fresh basil
30ml/2 tbsp pine nuts, toasted
fresh basil sprig, to garnish

For the dressing

90ml/6 tbsp olive oil
30ml/2 tbsp wine vinegar
5ml/1 tsp balsamic vinegar (optional)
5ml/1 tsp wholegrain mustard
pinch of sugar
salt and ground black pepper

1 Cook the pasta in plenty of boiling salted water according to the instructions on the packet. Drain well and cool.

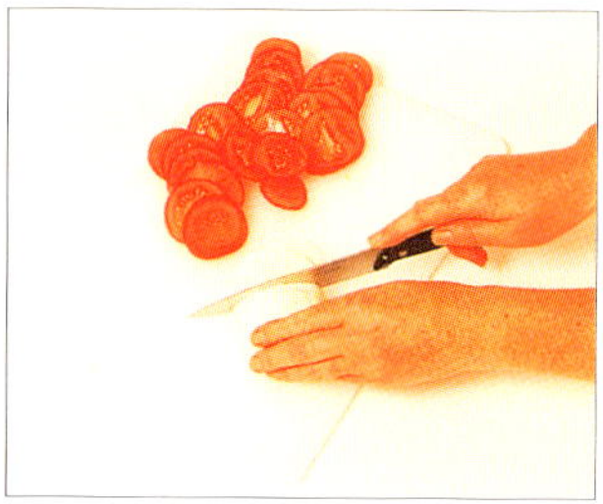

2 Using a sharp knife slice the tomatoes and mozzarella cheese into thin rounds.

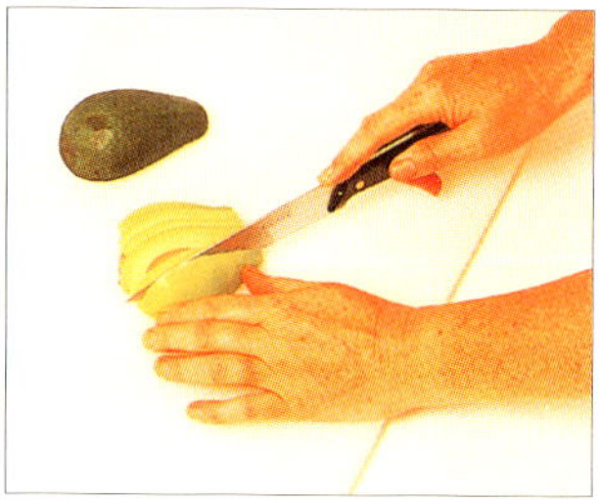

3 Halve the avocado, remove the stone and peel off the skin. Slice the flesh lengthways.

4 Place all the dressing ingredients together in a small bowl and whisk until well blended.

5 Arrange the sliced tomato, mozzarella and avocado overlapping around the edge of a flat serving plate.

6 Toss the pasta with half the dressing and the chopped basil. Pile into the centre of the plate. Pour over the remaining dressing, scatter over the pine nuts and garnish with a sprig of fresh basil. Serve immediately.

Sesame Noodle Salad with Hot Peanuts

An Orient-inspired salad with crunchy vegetables and a light soy dressing. The hot peanuts make a surprisingly successful union with the cold noodles.

INGREDIENTS

Serves 4

350g/12oz Chinese egg noodles
2 carrots, peeled and cut into fine julienne strips
½ cucumber, peeled and cut into 1cm/½in cubes
115g/4oz celeriac, peeled and cut into fine julienne strips
6 spring onions, finely sliced
8 canned water chestnuts, drained and finely sliced
175g/6oz beansprouts
1 small green chilli, seeded and finely chopped
30ml/2 tbsp sesame seeds, to serve
115g/4oz/1 cup peanuts, to serve

For the dressing

15ml/1 tbsp dark soy sauce
15ml/1 tbsp light soy sauce
15ml/1 tbsp clear honey
15ml/1 tbsp rice wine or dry sherry
15ml/1 tbsp sesame oil

1 Preheat the oven to 200°C/400°F/Gas 6. Cook the egg noodles in boiling water according to the instructions on the packet.

2 Drain the noodles, refresh in cold water, then drain again.

3 Mix the noodles with all of the prepared vegetables.

4 Combine the dressing ingredients in a small bowl, then toss into the noodle and vegetable mixture. Divide the salad among four serving plates.

5 Place the sesame seeds and peanuts on separate baking sheets and place in the oven. Take the sesame seeds out of the oven after 5 minutes and continue to cook the peanuts for a further 5 minutes until they are evenly browned.

6 Sprinkle the sesame seeds and peanuts evenly over each salad portion and serve at once.

Seafood Spaghetti

This sauce offers a real, fresh seafood flavour. Serve with hunks of crusty French bread.

INGREDIENTS

Serves 4

350g/12oz spaghetti
50g/2oz/¼ cup butter
1 onion, chopped
1 red pepper, cored, seeded and coarsely chopped
2 garlic cloves, chopped
15ml/1 tbsp paprika
450g/1lb live mussels in the shell
150ml/¼ pint/⅔ cup dry white wine
30ml/2 tbsp chopped fresh parsley
225g/8oz/2 cups peeled prawns
150ml/¼ pint/⅔ cup crème fraîche
salt and ground black pepper
finely chopped fresh flat leaf parsley, to garnish

1 Cook the pasta in plenty of boiling salted water according to the instructions on the packet.

2 Melt the butter in a frying pan and fry the onion, pepper, garlic and paprika for 5 minutes until almost softened.

3 Rinse and scrub the mussels, making sure all the shells are tightly shut or they close when tapped sharply with the back of a knife. Discard any open shells.

4 Add the wine to the pan and bring to the boil.

5 Stir in the mussels, parsley and prawns, cover and simmer for about 5 minutes until the mussels have opened. Discard any mussels that remain closed.

6 Using a slotted spoon, remove the shellfish from the pan and keep warm. Bring the juices back to the boil and boil rapidly until reduced by half.

7 Stir in the crème fraîche until well blended. Season to taste. Return the shellfish to the pan and simmer for 1 minute to heat them throughly.

8 Drain the pasta thoroughly and divide it among four serving plates. Spoon over the shellfish and serve, garnished with the finely chopped fresh flat leaf parsley.

Minestrone with Pesto Toasts

This Italian mixed vegetable soup comes originally from Genoa, but the vegetables vary from region to region. This is also a great way to use up leftover vegetables.

INGREDIENTS

Serves 4

30ml/2 tbsp olive oil
2 garlic cloves, crushed
1 onion, halved and sliced
225g/8oz lean bacon, diced
2 small courgettes, quartered and sliced
50g/2oz French beans, chopped
2 small carrots, diced
2 celery sticks, finely chopped
1 bouquet garni
50g/2oz short cut macaroni
50g/2oz/½ cup frozen peas
200g/7oz can kidney beans, drained and rinsed
50g/2oz/1 cup shredded green cabbage
4 tomatoes, skinned and seeded
salt and ground black pepper

For the toasts

8 slices French bread
15ml/1 tbsp ready-made pesto sauce
15ml/1 tbsp grated Parmesan cheese

1 Heat the oil in a large pan and gently fry the garlic and onions for 5 minutes, until just softened. Add the bacon, courgettes, French beans, carrots and celery to the pan and stir-fry for 3 minutes.

2 Pour 1.2 litres/2 pints/5 cups cold water over the vegetables and add the bouquet garni. Cover and simmer for 25 minutes.

3 Add the macaroni, peas and kidney beans and cook for 8 minutes.

4 Add the cabbage and tomatoes to the mixture and cook for a further 5 minutes.

5 Meanwhile, spread the bread slices with the pesto, sprinkle a little Parmesan over each one and brown lightly under a hot grill. Remove the bouquet garni, season and serve with the pesto toasts.

COOK'S TIP

To appeal to children you could replace the macaroni with coloured pasta shapes such as shells, twists or bows if you like.

Butter Bean and Pesto Pasta

Buy good quality, ready-made pesto, rather than making your own, if you prefer. Pesto forms the basis of many very tasty sauces, and is especially good with butter beans.

INGREDIENTS

Serves 4

225g/8oz pasta shapes
freshly grated nutmeg
30ml/2 tbsp extra virgin olive oil
400g/14oz can butter beans, drained
45ml/3 tbsp pesto sauce
150ml/¼ pint/⅔ cup single cream
salt and ground black pepper

To serve

45ml/3 tbsp pine nuts
grated cheese (optional)
fresh basil sprigs, to garnish (optional)

1 Cook the pasta in plenty of boiling salted water until *al dente*, then drain, leaving it a little wet. Return the pasta to the pan, season, and stir in the nutmeg and extra virgin olive oil.

2 Heat the beans in a saucepan with the pesto and cream, stirring until the mixture begins to simmer. Toss the beans and pesto into the pasta and mix well.

3 Serve in bowls topped with pine nuts, and add a little grated cheese and some fresh basil sprigs if you wish.

Mediterranean Salad with Basil

A type of Salade Niçoise with pasta, conjuring up all the sunny flavours of the Mediterranean.

INGREDIENTS

Serves 4

225g/8oz chunky pasta shapes
175g/6oz fine green beans
2 large ripe tomatoes
50g/2oz fresh basil leaves
200g/7oz can tuna fish in oil, drained
2 hard-boiled eggs, shelled and sliced or quartered
50g/2oz can anchovy fillets, drained
capers and black olives

For the dressing

90ml/6 tbsp extra virgin olive oil
30ml/2 tbsp white wine vinegar or lemon juice
2 garlic cloves, crushed
2.5ml/½ tsp Dijon mustard
30ml/2 tbsp chopped fresh basil
salt and ground black pepper

1 Whisk all the ingredients for the dressing together and leave to infuse while you make the salad.

2 Cook the pasta in plenty of boiling salted water according to the instructions on the packet. Drain well and cool.

3 Trim the beans and blanch in boiling salted water for about 3 minutes. Drain and refresh in cold water.

4 Slice or quarter the tomatoes and arrange in the base of a bowl. Moisten with a little dressing and cover with a quarter of the basil leaves. Then cover with the beans. Moisten with a little more dressing and cover with a third of the remaining basil.

5 Cover with the pasta tossed in a little more dressing and half the remaining basil. Roughly flake the tuna, then add to the bowl.

6 Arrange the eggs on top, then finally scatter over the anchovy fillets, capers and black olives. Pour over the remaining dressing and garnish with the remaining basil. Serve immediately. Don't be tempted to chill this salad – all the flavour will be dulled.

Pasta, Melon and Prawn Salad

Orange cantaloupe or Charentais melon look spectacular in this salad. Or try a mixture of ogen, cantaloupe and water melon.

INGREDIENTS

Serves 4–6

175g/6oz pasta shapes
225g/8oz/2 cups frozen prawns, thawed and drained
1 large or 2 small melons
60ml/4 tbsp olive oil
15ml/1 tbsp tarragon vinegar
30ml/2 tbsp snipped fresh chives or chopped parsley
herb sprigs, to garnish
shredded Chinese leaves, to serve

1 Cook the pasta in boiling salted water according to the instructions on the packet. Drain well and allow to cool.

2 Peel the prawns and discard the shells.

3 Halve the melon and remove the seeds with a teaspoon. Carefully scoop the flesh into balls with a melon baller and mix with the prawns and pasta.

4 Whisk the oil, vinegar and chopped herbs together. Pour on to the prawn mixture and turn to coat. Cover and chill for at least 30 minutes.

5 Meanwhile shred the Chinese leaves and use to line a shallow bowl or the empty melon halves.

6 Pile the prawn mixture on to the Chinese leaves and garnish with sprigs of herbs.

Chicken and Pasta Salad

This is a delicious way to use up leftover cooked chicken, and makes a filling meal.

INGREDIENTS

Serves 4

225g/8oz tri-coloured pasta twists
30ml/2 tbsp ready-made pesto sauce
15ml/1 tbsp olive oil
1 beefsteak tomato
12 stoned black olives
225g/8oz cooked French beans, cut into 4cm/1½in lengths
350g/12oz cooked chicken, cubed
salt and ground black pepper
fresh basil, to garnish

1 Cook the pasta in plenty of boiling salted water according to the instructions on the packet.

2 Drain the pasta and rinse in plenty of cold running water. Put into a bowl and stir in the pesto sauce and olive oil.

3 Skin the tomato by placing it in boiling water for about 45 seconds and then into cold water, to loosen the skin.

4 Cut the tomato into small cubes and add to the pasta with the olives, seasoning and French beans. Add the cubed chicken. Toss gently together and transfer to a serving platter. Garnish with fresh basil.

MIDWEEK MEALS

Aubergine Lasagne

This delicious lasagne is also suitable for home freezing.

INGREDIENTS

Serves 4

3 aubergines, sliced
75ml/5 tbsp olive oil
2 large onions, finely chopped
2 × 400g/14oz cans chopped tomatoes
5ml/1 tsp dried mixed herbs
2–3 garlic cloves, crushed
6 sheets no-precook lasagne
salt and ground black pepper

For the cheese sauce

25g/1oz/2 tbsp butter
25g/1oz/2 tbsp plain flour
300ml/½ pint/1¼ cups milk
2.5ml/½ tsp English mustard
115g/4oz/8 tbsp grated mature Cheddar
15g/½oz/1 tbsp grated Parmesan cheese

1 Layer the sliced aubergine in a colander, sprinkling lightly with salt between each layer. Leave to stand for 1 hour, then rinse and pat dry with kitchen paper.

2 Heat 60ml/4 tbsp of the oil in a large pan, fry the aubergine and drain on kitchen paper. Add the remaining oil to the pan, cook the onions for 5 minutes, then stir in the tomatoes, herbs, garlic and seasoning. Bring to the boil and simmer, covered, for 30 minutes.

3 Melt the butter in a pan, stir in the flour and cook gently for 1 minute, stirring. Gradually stir in the milk. Bring to the boil, stirring, and cook for 2 minutes. Remove from the heat and stir in the mustard, cheeses and seasoning.

4 Preheat the oven to 200°C/400°F/Gas 6. Arrange half the aubergines in the base of an ovenproof dish, spoon over half the tomato sauce. Arrange three sheets of lasagne on top. Repeat.

5 Spoon over the cheese sauce, cover and bake for 30 minutes until lightly browned.

Macaroni Soufflé

This is generally a great favourite with children, and is rather like a light and fluffy macaroni cheese. Make sure you serve the soufflé immediately after it is cooked or it will sink dramatically.

INGREDIENTS

Serves 3–4

75g/3oz short cut macaroni
melted butter, to coat
25g/1oz/3 tbsp dried breadcrumbs
50g/2oz/4 tbsp butter
5ml/1 tsp ground paprika
40g/1½oz/⅓ cup plain flour
300ml/½ pint/1¼ cups milk
75g/3oz Cheddar or Gruyère cheese, grated
50g/2oz Parmesan cheese, grated
3 eggs, separated
salt and ground black pepper

1 Cook the macaroni in plenty of boiling salted water according to the instructions on the packet. Drain well and set aside. Preheat the oven to 150°C/300°F/Gas 2.

2 Brush a 1.2 litre/2 pint/5 cup soufflé dish with melted butter, then coat evenly with the breadcrumbs, shaking out any excess from the pan.

3 Put the butter, paprika, flour and milk into a saucepan and slowly bring to the boil, whisking constantly until the mixture is smooth and thick.

4 Simmer the sauce for 1 minute, then remove from the heat and stir in the cheeses until melted. Season well and mix with the cooked macaroni.

5 Beat in the egg yolks. Whisk the egg whites until they form soft peaks and spoon a quarter into the sauce mixture to lighten it slightly.

6 Using a large metal spoon, carefully fold in the rest of the egg whites and transfer to the prepared soufflé dish.

7 Bake in the centre of the oven for about 40–45 minutes until the soufflé is risen and golden brown. The middle should wobble very slightly and the soufflé should be lightly creamy inside.

Greek Pasta Bake

Another excellent main meal (called pastitsio *in Greece), this recipe is both economical and filling.*

INGREDIENTS

Serves 4

15ml/1 tbsp oil
450g/1lb/4 cups minced lamb
1 onion, chopped
2 garlic cloves, crushed
30ml/2 tbsp tomato purée
25g/1oz/2 tbsp plain flour
300ml/½ pint/1¼ cups lamb stock
2 large tomatoes
115g/4oz/1 cup pasta shapes
450g/1lb tub Greek yogurt
2 eggs
salt and ground black pepper

1 Preheat the oven to 190°C/375°F/Gas 5. Heat the oil in a large pan and fry the lamb for 5 minutes. Add the onion and garlic and continue to fry for a further 5 minutes.

2 Stir the tomato purée and flour into the pan. Cook for a further 1 minute.

3 Stir in the stock and season to taste. Bring to the boil and cook for 20 minutes.

4 Slice the tomatoes, place the meat in an ovenproof dish and arrange the tomatoes on top.

5 Cook the pasta shapes in boiling salted water for about 8–10 minutes or until *al dente*. Drain thoroughly.

6 Mix together the pasta, yogurt and eggs. Spoon on top of the tomatoes and then cook in the preheated oven for 1 hour. Serve with a crisp salad, if desired.

Bolognese Meat Sauce

This great meat sauce is a speciality of Bologna. It is delicious with tagliatelle or short pastas such as penne or conchiglie as well as spaghetti, and is indispensable in baked lasagne. It keeps well in the fridge for several days and can also be frozen for up to three months.

INGREDIENTS

Serves 6

25g/1oz/2 tbsp butter
60ml/4 tbsp olive oil
1 onion, finely chopped
25g/1oz/2 tbsp finely chopped pancetta or unsmoked bacon
1 carrot, finely sliced
1 celery stick, finely sliced
1 garlic clove, finely chopped
350g/12oz/3 cups lean minced beef
150ml/¼ pint/⅔ cup red wine
120ml/4fl oz/½ cup milk
400g/14oz can plum tomatoes, chopped, with their juice
1 bay leaf
1.5ml/¼ tsp fresh thyme leaves
salt and ground black pepper
cooked pasta, to serve

1 Heat the butter and oil in a heavy-based saucepan. Add the onion, and cook over a moderate heat for 3–4 minutes. Add the pancetta or bacon, and cook until the onion is translucent. Stir in the carrot, celery and garlic. Cook for a further 3–4 minutes.

2 Add the beef, and crumble it into the vegetables with a fork. Stir until the meat loses its red colour. Season to taste.

3 Pour in the wine, increase the heat slightly, and cook until the liquid evaporates, about 3–4 minutes. Add the milk and cook until it has evaporated.

4 Stir in the tomatoes with their juice, and the herbs. Bring the sauce to the boil. Reduce the heat to low and simmer, uncovered, for 1½–2 hours, stirring occasionally. Correct the seasoning before serving on a bed of pasta.

Pasta Carbonara

An Italian favourite, carbonara is traditionally served with spaghetti, but it is equally delicious made with fresh egg tagliatelle.

INGREDIENTS

Serves 4

350–450g/12oz–1lb fresh tagliatelle
15ml/1 tbsp olive oil
225g/8oz ham, bacon or pancetta, cut into 2.5cm/1in sticks
115g/4oz button mushrooms, sliced
4 eggs, lightly beaten
75ml/5 tbsp single cream
30ml/2 tbsp finely grated Parmesan cheese
salt and ground black pepper
fresh basil sprigs, to garnish

1 Cook the pasta in a pan of boiling salted water, with a little oil added, for 3–5 minutes or until *al dente.*

2 Meanwhile, heat the oil in a frying pan and add the meat. Fry for 3–4 minutes and then add the mushrooms and fry for a further 3–4 minutes. Turn off the heat and reserve. Lightly beat the eggs and cream together in a bowl and season well.

3 When the pasta is cooked, drain it well and return to the pan. Stir in the meat, mushrooms and any pan juices.

4 Pour in the eggs, cream and half the Parmesan cheese. Stir well and as you do this the eggs will cook in the heat of the pasta. Pile on to warmed serving plates, sprinkle with the remaining Parmesan and garnish with basil.

Pasta Bake

A popular British supper dish – replace the Cheddar with your family's favourite cheese.

INGREDIENTS

Serves 4

15ml/1 tbsp olive oil
275g/10oz macaroni
2 leeks, chopped
50g/2oz/4 tbsp butter
50g/2oz/½ cup plain flour
900ml/1½ pints/3¾ cups milk
225g/8oz/2 cups grated mature Cheddar cheese
30ml/2 tbsp fromage frais
5ml/1 tsp wholegrain mustard
50g/2oz/1 cup fresh breadcrumbs
25g/1oz/½ cup grated Double Gloucester cheese
salt and ground black pepper
15ml/1 tbsp chopped fresh parsley, to garnish

1 Preheat the oven to 180°C/350°F/Gas 4. Bring a large pan of salted water to the boil and add the olive oil. Then add the macaroni and leeks and boil gently for 10 minutes. Drain, rinse under cold water and reserve.

2 Heat the butter in a saucepan, stir in the flour and cook for about 1 minute. Remove from the heat and gradually add the milk, stirring well after each addition, until smooth. Return to the heat and stir continuously until the sauce is thickened.

3 Add the Cheddar cheese, fromage frais and mustard, mix well, and season with salt and ground black pepper.

4 Stir the drained macaroni and leeks into the cheese sauce and pile into a greased ovenproof dish. Level the top with the back of a spoon and sprinkle over the breadcrumbs and the grated Double Gloucester cheese.

5 Bake for 35–40 minutes. Serve hot, garnished with chopped fresh parsley.

Turkey Pastitsio

A traditional Greek pastitsio is made with minced beef, but this lighter version is just as tasty.

INGREDIENTS

Serves 4–6

450g/1lb/4 cups lean minced turkey
1 large onion, finely chopped
60ml/4 tbsp tomato purée
250ml/8fl oz/1 cup red wine or stock
5ml/1 tsp ground cinnamon
300g/11oz macaroni
300ml/½ pint/1¼ cups skimmed milk
25g/1oz/2 tbsp sunflower margarine
25g/1oz/3 tbsp plain flour
5ml/1 tsp grated nutmeg
2 tomatoes, sliced
60ml/4 tbsp wholemeal breadcrumbs
salt and ground black pepper
green salad, to serve

1 Preheat the oven to 220°C/425°F/Gas 7. Fry the turkey and onion in a non-stick pan without any fat, stirring until lightly browned.

2 Stir in the tomato purée, red wine or stock and cinnamon. Season, then cover and simmer for about 5 minutes.

3 Cook the macaroni in plenty of boiling salted water according to the instructions on the packet, until just tender, then drain.

4 Layer with the turkey mixture in a wide ovenproof dish.

5 Place the milk, margarine and flour in a saucepan and whisk over a moderate heat until thickened and smooth.

6 Whisk the nutmeg and seasoning to taste into the sauce, then pour evenly over the pasta. Arrange the tomato slices on top and sprinkle with lines of breadcrumbs.

7 Bake for 30–35 minutes, or until golden brown.

Fusilli with Turkey

Broccoli combines with the other ingredients to make a one-pan meal.

INGREDIENTS

Serves 4

675g/1½lb ripe, firm plum tomatoes, quartered
90ml/6 tbsp olive oil
5ml/1 tsp dried oregano
350g/12oz broccoli florets
1 small onion, sliced
5ml/1 tsp dried thyme
450g/1lb skinless, boneless turkey breast, cubed
3 garlic cloves, crushed
15ml/1 tbsp fresh lemon juice
450g/1lb fusilli
salt and ground black pepper

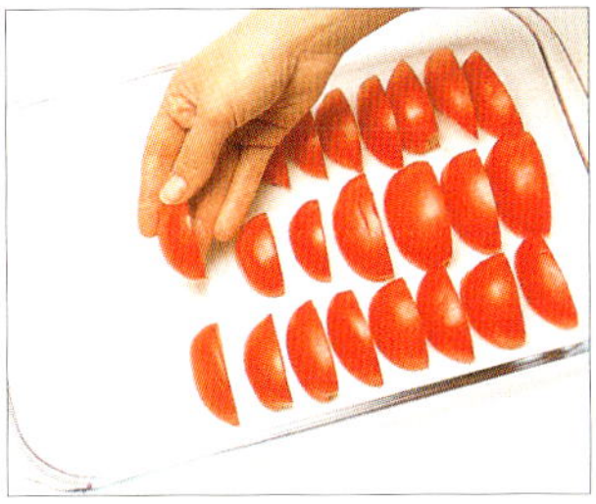

1 Preheat the oven to 200°C/400°F/Gas 6. Place the plum tomatoes in a baking dish. Add 15ml/1 tbsp of the oil, the oregano and 2.5ml/½ tsp salt and stir.

2 Bake for 30–40 minutes, until the tomatoes are just browned; do not stir.

3 Meanwhile, bring a large saucepan of salted water to the boil. Add the broccoli florets and cook until just tender, about 5 minutes. Drain and set aside. (Alternatively, steam the broccoli until tender.)

4 Heat 30ml/2 tbsp of the oil in a large non-stick frying pan. Add the onion, thyme, turkey and 2.5ml/½ tsp salt. Cook over a high heat, stirring often, until the meat is cooked and beginning to brown, about 5–7 minutes. Add the garlic and cook for a further 1 minute, stirring frequently.

5 Remove from the heat. Stir in the lemon juice and season with ground black pepper. Set aside and keep warm.

6 Cook the fusilli in plenty of boiling salted water according to the instructions on the packet until *al dente*. Drain and place in a large bowl. Toss the pasta with the remaining oil.

7 Add the broccoli to the turkey mixture, then stir into the fusilli. Add the tomatoes and stir gently to blend. Serve immediately.

Noodles with Italian Mushrooms

Porcini mushrooms give this sauce a wonderful depth.

INGREDIENTS

Serves 2–4

25g/1oz dried Italian mushrooms (porcini)
175ml/6fl oz/¾ cup warm water
900g/2lb tomatoes, peeled, seeded and chopped or drained canned tomatoes
1.5ml/¼ tsp dried hot chilli flakes
45ml/3 tbsp olive oil
4 slices pancetta or rashers unsmoked back bacon, cut into thin strips
1 large garlic clove, finely chopped
350g/12oz tagliatelle or fettuccine
salt and ground black pepper
freshly grated Parmesan cheese, to serve

1 Put the mushrooms in a bowl and cover with the warm water. Leave to soak for 20 minutes.

2 Meanwhile, put the tomatoes in a saucepan with the chilli flakes and seasoning. If using canned tomatoes, crush them coarsely with a fork or potato masher. Bring to the boil, reduce the heat and simmer for about 30–40 minutes, until reduced to 750ml/1¼ pints/3 cups. Stir from time to time to prevent sticking.

3 When the mushrooms have finished soaking, lift them out and squeeze the remaining liquid over the bowl; set aside.

4 Carefully pour the soaking liquid into the tomatoes through a muslin-lined sieve. Simmer the tomatoes for a further 15 minutes.

5 Meanwhile, heat 30ml/2 tbsp of the oil in a frying pan. Add the strips of pancetta or bacon and fry until golden but not crisp. Add the garlic and mushrooms and fry for 3 minutes, stirring. Set aside.

6 Cook the pasta in plenty of boiling salted water until just *al dente.*

7 Add the bacon and mushroom mixture to the tomato sauce and mix well. Season with salt and ground black pepper.

8 Drain the pasta and return to the pan. Add the remaining oil and toss to coat the strands. Divide among hot plates, spoon the sauce on top and serve with freshly grated Parmesan cheese.

Chicken Lasagne

Based on the Italian beef lasagne, this is an excellent dish for entertaining guests of all ages. Serve simply with a green salad.

INGREDIENTS

Serves 8

30ml/2 tbsp olive oil
900g/2lb/8 cups minced raw chicken
225g/8oz rindless streaky bacon rashers, chopped
2 garlic cloves, crushed
450g/1lb leeks, sliced
225g/8oz carrots, diced
30ml/2 tbsp tomato purée
450ml/¾ pint/1¾ cups chicken stock
12 sheets (no-precook) green lasagne

For the cheese sauce

50g/2oz/4 tbsp butter
50g/2oz/4 tbsp plain flour
600ml/1 pint/2½ cups milk
115g/4oz/1 cup grated mature Cheddar cheese
1.5ml/¼ tsp English mustard powder
salt and ground black pepper

1 Heat the oil in a large flameproof casserole and brown the minced chicken and bacon briskly, separating the pieces with a wooden spoon. Add the crushed garlic cloves, chopped leeks and diced carrots and cook for about 5 minutes until softened. Add the tomato purée, stock and seasoning. Bring to the boil, cover and simmer for 30 minutes.

2 For the sauce, melt the butter in a saucepan, add the flour and gradually blend in the milk, stirring until smooth. Bring to the boil, stirring all the time until thickened, and simmer for several minutes. Add half the grated Cheddar cheese and the mustard and season to taste.

3 Preheat the oven to 190°C/375°F/Gas 5. Layer the chicken mixture, lasagne and half the cheese sauce in a 2.5 litre/5 pint/12 cup ovenproof dish, starting and finishing with the chicken mixture.

4 Pour over the remaining cheese sauce, sprinkle over the remaining cheese and bake in the preheated oven for 1 hour, or until lightly browned.

Cannelloni Stuffed with Meat

Cannelloni are rectangles of home-made egg pasta which are spread with a filling, rolled up and baked in a sauce. In this recipe, they are baked in a béchamel sauce.

INGREDIENTS

Serves 6–8

30ml/2 tbsp olive oil
1 onion, very finely chopped
225g/8oz/1½ cups very lean minced beef
75g/3oz/½ cup finely chopped cooked ham
15ml/1 tbsp chopped fresh parsley
30ml/2 tbsp tomato purée, softened in 15ml/1 tbsp warm water
1 egg
egg pasta sheets made with 2 eggs
750ml/1¼ pints/3 cups béchamel sauce
50g/2oz/½ cup freshly grated Parmesan cheese
40g/11/2oz/3 tbsp butter
salt and ground black pepper

1 Prepare the meat filling by heating the oil in a medium saucepan. Add the onion and sauté gently until translucent. Stir in the beef, crumbling it with a fork, and stirring constantly until it has lost its raw red colour. Cook for about 3–4 minutes.

2 Remove from the heat and turn the beef mixture into a bowl with the ham and parsley. Add the tomato purée mixture and the egg, and mix well. Season with salt and pepper. Set aside.

3 Make the egg pasta sheets. Do not let the pasta dry before cutting it into rectangles, about 13–15cm/5–6in long and as wide as they come from the machine (7.5cm/3in if you are not using a pasta machine).

4 Bring a very large pan of water to the boil. Place a large bowl of cold water near the cooker. Cover a large work surface with a tablecloth. Add salt to the rapidly boiling water. Drop in three or four of the egg pasta rectangles. Cook very briefly, for about 30 seconds. Plunge them into the cold water, shake off the excess and lay them out flat on the tablecloth. Continue until all the pasta has been cooked in this way.

5 Preheat the oven to 220°C/425°F/Gas 7. Select a shallow baking dish large enough to take all the cannelloni in one layer. Butter the dish and smear about 30–45ml/2–3 tbsp of béchamel sauce over the base.

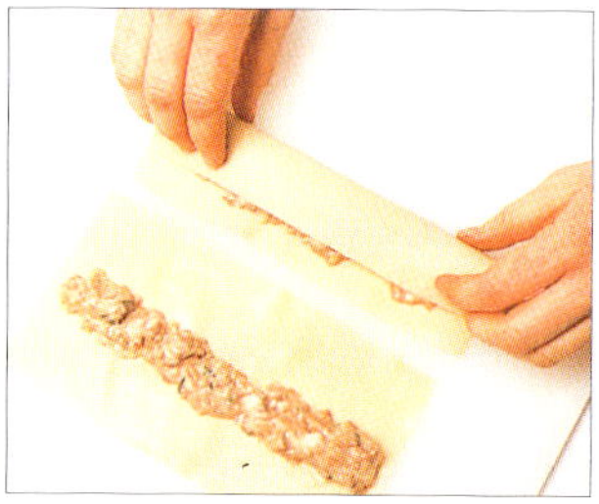

6 Stir about one-third of the sauce into the meat filling. Spread a thin layer of filling on each pasta rectangle. Roll the rectangles up loosely starting from a long side, Swiss-roll style. Place the cannelloni in the baking dish with their open edges underneath.

7 Spoon the rest of the sauce over the cannelloni, pushing a little down between each pasta roll. Sprinkle the top with the grated Parmesan and dot with butter. Bake for about 20 minutes. Allow to rest for 5–8 minutes before serving on warmed plates.

Cheesy Pasta Bolognese

Mozzarella gives the cheese sauce a particularly creamy taste.

INGREDIENTS

Serves 4

30ml/2 tbsp olive oil
1 onion, chopped
1 garlic clove, crushed
1 carrot, diced
2 celery sticks, chopped
2 rashers streaky bacon, finely chopped
5 button mushrooms, chopped
450g/1lb lean minced beef
120ml/4fl oz/½ cup red wine
15ml/1 tbsp tomato purée
200g/7oz can chopped tomatoes
fresh thyme sprig
225g/8oz dried penne
300ml/½ pint/1¼ cups milk
25g/1oz/2 tbsp butter
25g/1oz/2 tbsp flour
150g/5oz/1 cup cubed mozzarella cheese
60ml/4 tbsp grated Parmesan cheese
salt and ground black pepper
fresh basil sprigs, to garnish

1 Heat the oil in a pan and fry the onion, garlic, carrot and celery for 6 minutes, until the onions have softened.

2 Add the bacon and continue frying for 3–4 minutes. Stir in the mushrooms, fry for 2 minutes, then add the beef. Fry over a high heat until well browned all over.

3 Pour in the red wine, the tomato purée dissolved in 45ml/3 tbsp water, and the tomatoes, then add the thyme and season well. Bring to the boil, cover the pan and simmer gently for about 30 minutes.

4 Preheat the oven to 200°C/400°F/Gas 6. Bring a pan of water to the boil, add a little oil. Cook the pasta for 10 minutes.

5 Meanwhile, place the milk, butter and flour in a saucepan, heat gently and whisk constantly with a balloon whisk until the mixture is thickened. Stir in the cubed mozzarella cheese, 30ml/2 tbsp of the Parmesan and season lightly.

6 Drain the pasta and stir into the cheese sauce. Uncover the tomato sauce and boil rapidly for about 2 minutes to reduce.

7 Spoon the sauce into an ovenproof dish, top with the pasta mixture and sprinkle the remaining 30ml/2 tbsp Parmesan cheese evenly over the top. Bake for 25 minutes until golden. Garnish with basil and serve hot.

Thai Fried Noodles

An amazing array of tastes and textures make up this dish.

INGREDIENTS

Serves 4

225g/8oz thread egg noodles
60ml/4 tbsp vegetable oil
2 garlic cloves, finely chopped
175g/6oz pork tenderloin, sliced into thin strips
1 skinless boneless chicken breast, about 175g/6oz, sliced into thin strips
115g/4oz/1 cup cooked peeled shrimps (rinsed if canned)
45ml/3 tbsp lime or lemon juice
45ml/3 tbsp oriental fish sauce
30ml/2 tbsp soft light brown sugar
2 eggs, beaten
½ red chilli, seeded and finely chopped
50g/2oz/¼ cup beansprouts
60ml/4 tbsp roasted peanuts, chopped
3 spring onions, cut into 5cm/2in lengths and shredded
45ml/3 tbsp chopped fresh coriander

1 Place the noodles in a large pan of boiling water and leave to stand for about 5 minutes.

2 Meanwhile, heat 45ml/3 tbsp of the oil in a wok or large frying pan, add the garlic and cook for 30 seconds. Add the pork and chicken and stir-fry over a high heat until lightly browned, then add the shrimps and stir-fry for a further 2 minutes.

3 Add the lime or lemon juice, fish sauce and sugar, and stir-fry until the sugar has dissolved.

4 Drain the noodles and add to the pan with the remaining 15ml/1 tbsp oil. Toss all the ingredients together.

5 Pour in the beaten eggs. Stir-fry until almost set, then add the chilli and beansprouts. Divide the peanuts, spring onions and coriander leaves into two and add half to the pan. Stir-fry for

2 minutes, then tip the mixture on to a serving platter. Sprinkle on the remaining peanuts, spring onions and coriander and serve the noodles at once.

Rigatoni with Spicy Sausage

This is really a cheat's Bolognese sauce using the wonderful fresh spicy sausages sold in every good Italian delicatessen.

INGREDIENTS

Serves 4

450g/1lb fresh spicy Italian sausage
30ml/2 tbsp olive oil
1 onion, chopped
450ml/¾ pint/1¾ cups passata
150ml/¼ pint/⅔ cup dry red wine
6 sun-dried tomatoes in oil, drained
450g/1lb rigatoni or similar pasta
salt and ground black pepper
freshly grated Parmesan cheese, to serve

1 Squeeze the sausages out of their skins into a bowl and break up the meat.

2 Heat the oil in a medium saucepan and add the onion. Cook for 5 minutes until soft and golden. Stir in the sausagemeat, browning it all over and breaking up the lumps with a wooden spoon. Pour in the passata and the wine. Bring to the boil.

3 Slice the sun-dried tomatoes and add to the sauce. Simmer for 3 minutes until reduced, stirring occasionally. Season.

4 Cook the pasta in plenty of boiling salted water according to the instructions on the packet. Drain well and top with the sauce. Serve with Parmesan cheese.

Pasta with Tomato and Smoky Bacon

A wonderful sauce to prepare in mid-summer when the tomatoes are ripe and sweet.

INGREDIENTS

Serves 4

900g/2lb ripe tomatoes
6 rashers smoked streaky bacon
50g/2oz/4 tbsp butter
1 onion, chopped
15ml/1 tbsp chopped fresh oregano or 5ml/1 tsp dried
450g/1lb pasta, any variety
salt and ground black pepper
freshly grated Parmesan cheese, to serve

1 Plunge the tomatoes into boiling water for 1 minute, then into cold water. Slip off the skins. Halve the tomatoes, remove the seeds and cores and roughly chop the flesh.

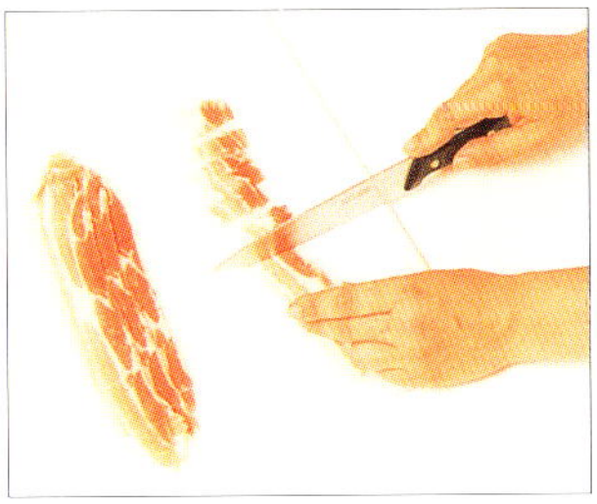

2 Remove the rind from the streaky bacon and roughly chop the meat.

3 Melt the butter in a saucepan and add the bacon. Fry until lightly browned, then add the onion and cook gently for 5 minutes until softened. Add the tomatoes, salt, pepper and oregano. Simmer gently for 10 minutes.

4 Cook the pasta in plenty of boiling salted water according to the instructions on the packet. Drain well and toss with the sauce. Serve with plenty of freshly grated Parmesan cheese.

Rotolo di Pasta

A giant Swiss roll of pasta with a spinach filling, which is poached, sliced and baked with béchamel or tomato sauce. Use fresh homemade pasta for this recipe, or ask your local Italian deli to make a large sheet of pasta for you!

INGREDIENTS

Serves 6

700g/1½lb frozen chopped spinach, thawed
50g/2oz/4 tbsp butter
1 onion, chopped
100g/4oz ham or bacon, diced
225g/8oz ricotta or curd cheese
1 egg
freshly grated nutmeg
fresh spinach pasta made with 2 eggs and 200g/7oz/1¾ cups flour
1.2 litres/2 pints/5 cups béchamel sauce, warmed
50g/2oz/½ cup freshly grated Parmesan cheese
salt and ground black pepper

1 Squeeze the excess moisture from the spinach and set aside.

2 Melt the butter in a saucepan and fry the onion until golden. Add the ham and fry until beginning to brown. Take off the heat and stir in the spinach. Cool slightly, then beat in the ricotta or curd cheese and the egg. Season with salt, pepper and nutmeg.

3 Roll the pasta out to a rectangle about 30 × 40cm/12 × 16in. Spread the filling all over, leaving a 1cm/½in border all round the edge of the rectangle.

4 Roll up from the shorter end and wrap in muslin to form a "sausage", tying the ends securely with string. Poach in a very large pan (or fish kettle) of simmering water for 20 minutes or until firm. Carefully remove, drain and then unwrap. Leave to cool.

5 When you are ready to finish the dish, preheat the oven to 200°C/400°F/Gas 6. Cut the pasta roll into 2.5cm/1in slices. Spoon a little béchamel sauce over the base of a shallow baking dish and arrange the slices on top, slightly overlapping each other.

6 Spoon over the remaining sauce, sprinkle with the cheese and bake for 15–20 minutes or until browned and bubbling. Allow to stand for a few minutes before serving.

Pasta Timbales

An alternative way to serve pasta for a special occasion. Mixed with minced beef and tomato and baked in a lettuce parcel, it makes an impressive dish for a dinner party.

INGREDIENTS

Serves 4

8 cos lettuce leaves

For the filling

15ml/1 tbsp oil
175g/6oz/1½ cups minced beef
15ml/1 tbsp tomato purée
1 garlic clove, crushed
115g/4oz macaroni
salt and ground black pepper

For the sauce

25g/1oz/2 tbsp butter
25g/1oz/2 tbsp plain flour
250ml/8fl oz/1 cup double cream
30ml/2 tbsp chopped fresh basil

1 Preheat the oven to 180°C/350°F/Gas 4. For the filling, heat the oil in a large pan and fry the minced beef for 7 minutes. Add the tomato purée and garlic and cook for 5 minutes.

2 Cook the macaroni in boiling salted water for 8–10 minutes or until *al dente*. Drain.

3 Mix together the pasta and minced beef mixture.

4 Line four 150ml/¼ pint/⅔ cup ramekin dishes with the cos lettuce leaves. Season the mince and spoon into the lettuce-lined ramekins.

5 Fold the lettuce leaves over the filling and place in a roasting tin half-filled with boiling water. Cover and cook for 20 minutes.

6 For the sauce melt the butter in a pan. Add the flour and cook for 1 minute. Stir in the cream and fresh basil. Season and bring to the boil, stirring all the time. Turn out the timbales and serve with the creamy basil sauce, and a crisp green salad if liked.

Spaghetti alla Carbonara

It has been said that this dish was originally cooked by Italian coal miners or charcoal-burners, hence the name "carbonara". The secret of its creamy sauce is not to overcook the egg.

INGREDIENTS

Serves 4

175g/6oz unsmoked streaky bacon
1 garlic clove, chopped
3 eggs
450g/1lb spaghetti
60ml/4 tbsp freshly grated Parmesan cheese
salt and ground black pepper

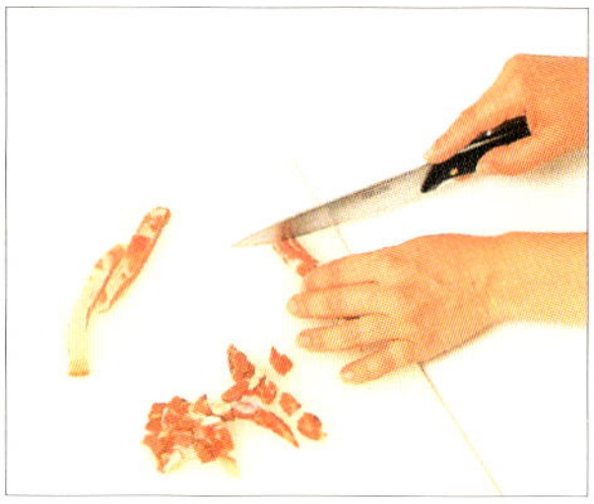

1 Dice the bacon and place in a medium saucepan. Fry in its own fat with the garlic until brown. Keep warm until needed.

2 Whisk the eggs together in a mixing bowl.

3 Cook the spaghetti in plenty of boiling salted water according to the instructions on the packet or until *al dente*. Drain well.

4 Quickly turn the spaghetti into the pan with the bacon and stir in the eggs, a little salt, lots of pepper and half the cheese. Toss well to mix. The eggs should half-cook in the heat from the pasta. Serve in warmed bowls with the remaining Parmesan cheese sprinkled over each portion.

Pasta with Bolognese Sauce

Traditional Bolognese sauce contains chicken livers to add richness, but you can leave them out and replace with an equal quantity of minced beef.

INGREDIENTS

Serves 4–6

75g/3oz pancetta or bacon
115g/4oz chicken livers
50g/2oz/4 tbsp butter, plus extra for tossing the pasta
1 onion, finely chopped
1 carrot, diced
1 celery stick, finely chopped
225g/8oz/2 cups lean minced beef
30ml/2 tbsp tomato purée
120ml/4fl oz/½ cup white wine
200ml/7fl oz/scant 1 cup beef stock or water
freshly grated nutmeg
450g/1lb tagliatelle, spaghetti or fettuccine
salt and ground black pepper
freshly grated Parmesan cheese, to serve

1 Dice the pancetta or bacon. Trim the chicken livers, removing any fat or gristle and any "green" bits which will be bitter if left on. Roughly chop the livers.

2 Melt 50g/2oz/4 tbsp butter in a saucepan and add the bacon. Cook for 2-3 minutes until just beginning to brown. Then add the onion, carrot and celery and brown these too.

3 Stir in the beef and brown over a high heat, breaking it up with a spoon. Add the chicken livers and cook for 2-3 minutes. Add the tomato purée with the wine and stock or water. Season well with salt, pepper and nutmeg. Bring to the boil, cover and simmer for 35 minutes.

4 Cook the pasta in plenty of boiling salted water according to the instructions on the packet or until *al dente*. Drain well and toss with the extra butter. Toss the meat sauce with the pasta and serve with plenty of grated Parmesan cheese.

Home-made Ravioli

It is a pleasure to make your own fresh pasta and you might be surprised at just how easy it is to fill and shape ravioli. Allow a little more time than you would for ready-made or dried pasta. A blender or food processor will save you time and effort in making and kneading the dough. A pasta-making machine helps with the rolling out, but both these jobs can be done by hand if necessary.

INGREDIENTS

Serves 6

200g/7oz/1¾ cups strong plain flour
5ml/½ tsp salt
15ml/1 tbsp olive oil
2 eggs, beaten

For the filling

1 small red onion, finely chopped
1 small green pepper, finely chopped
1 carrot, coarsely grated
15ml/1 tbsp olive oil
50g/2oz/½ cup walnuts, chopped
115g/4oz/½ cup ricotta cheese
30ml/2 tbsp freshly grated Parmesan or pecorino cheese
15ml/1 tbsp chopped fresh marjoram or basil
salt and ground black pepper
extra oil or melted butter, to serve

1 Sift the flour and salt into a blender or food processor. With the machine running, trickle in the oil and eggs and blend to a stiff but smooth dough.

2 Allow the machine to run for at least 1 minute if possible, otherwise remove the dough and knead by hand for 5 minutes.

3 If you are using a pasta machine, break off small balls of dough and feed them through the rollers, several times, according to the instructions that come with the machine.

4 If rolling the pasta by hand, divide the dough into two and roll out on a lightly floured surface to a thickness of about 5mm/¼in.

5 Fold the pasta into three and re-roll. Repeat this up to six times until the dough is smooth and no longer sticky. Roll the pasta slightly more thinly each time.

6 Keep the rolled dough under clean, dry dish towels while you complete the rest and make the filling. You should aim to have an even number of pasta sheets, all the same size.

7 Fry the onion, pepper and carrot in the oil for 5 minutes, then allow to cool. Mix with the walnuts, cheeses, herbs and lots of seasoning.

8 Lay out a pasta sheet and place small scoops of the filling in neat rows about 5cm/2in apart. Brush between the mounds of filling with a little water and then place another pasta sheet on the top to cover.

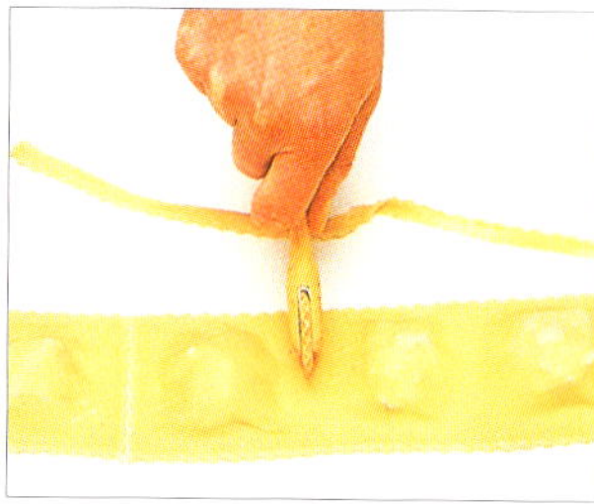

9 Press down well in between the rows then, using a ravioli or pastry cutter, cut into squares. If the edges pop open, press them back gently with your fingers.

10 Leave the ravioli to dry in the fridge, then boil in plenty of lightly salted water for just 5 minutes.

11 Toss the cooked ravioli in a little oil or melted butter before serving with homemade tomato sauce or extra cheese.

Autumn Glory

Glorious pumpkin shells summon up the delights of autumn and seem too good simply to throw away. Use one instead as a serving dish. Pumpkin and pasta make marvellous partners, especially as a main course served from the baked shell.

INGREDIENTS

Serves 4

1.75kg/4–4½lb pumpkin
1 onion, sliced
2.5cm/1in piece fresh root ginger
45ml/3 tbsp extra virgin olive oil
1 courgette, sliced
115g/4oz sliced mushrooms
400g/14oz can chopped tomatoes
75g/3oz pasta shells
450ml/¾ pint/1¾ cups stock
60ml/4 tbsp fromage frais
30ml/2 tbsp chopped fresh basil
salt and ground black pepper

1 Preheat the oven to 180°C/350°F/Gas 4. Cut the top off the pumpkin with a large, sharp knife and scoop out and discard the pumpkin seeds.

2 Using a small sharp knife and a sturdy tablespoon, cut and scrape out as much flesh from the pumpkin shell as possible, then chop the flesh into rough chunks.

3 Bake the pumpkin with its lid on for 45 minutes–1 hour until the inside begins to soften.

4 Meanwhile, make the filling. Gently fry the onion, ginger and pumpkin flesh in the olive oil for about 10 minutes, stirring the mixture occasionally.

5 Add the sliced courgette and mushrooms and cook for a further 3 minutes, then stir in the tomatoes, pasta shells and stock. Season well, bring to the boil, then cover the pan and simmer gently for about 10 minutes.

6 Stir the fromage frais and basil into the pasta and spoon the mixture into the pumpkin. It may not be possible to fit all the filling into the pumpkin shell, so serve the rest separately if necessary.

Pasta with Caponata

The Sicilians have an excellent sweet-and-sour vegetable dish, called caponata, *which goes wonderfully well with pasta.*

INGREDIENTS

Serves 4

1 aubergine, cut into sticks
2 courgettes, cut into sticks
8 baby onions, peeled or 1 large onion, sliced
2 garlic cloves, crushed
1 large red pepper, sliced
60ml/4 tbsp olive oil, preferably extra virgin
450ml/¾ pint/1¾ cups tomato juice
150ml/¼ pint/⅔ cup water
30ml/2 tbsp balsamic vinegar
juice of 1 lemon
15ml/1 tbsp sugar
30ml/2 tbsp sliced black olives
30ml/2 tbsp capers
400g/14oz tagliatelle or other ribbon pasta
salt and ground black pepper

1 Lightly salt the aubergine and courgettes and leave them to drain in a colander for 30 minutes. Rinse and pat dry thoroughly with kitchen paper.

2 In a large saucepan, lightly fry the onions, garlic and pepper in the oil for 5 minutes, then stir in the aubergine and courgettes and fry for a further 5 minutes.

3 Stir in the tomato juice and the water. Stir well, bring the mixture to the boil, then add all the rest of the ingredients except the pasta. Season to taste and simmer for 10 minutes.

4 Meanwhile, cook the pasta according to the instructions on the packet, then drain. Serve the *caponata* with the pasta.

Broccoli and Ricotta Cannelloni

This dish will be enjoyed by both vegetarians and meat-eaters.

INGREDIENTS

Serves 4

12 dried cannelloni tubes, 7.5cm/3in long
450g/1lb/4 cups broccoli florets
75g/3oz/1½ cups fresh breadcrumbs
150ml/¼ pint/⅔ cup milk
60ml/4 tbsp olive oil, plus extra for brushing
225g/8oz/1 cup ricotta cheese
pinch of grated nutmeg
90ml/6 tbsp grated Parmesan or pecorino cheese
salt and ground black pepper
30ml/2 tbsp pine nuts, for sprinkling

For the tomato sauce

30ml/2 tbsp olive oil
1 onion, finely chopped
1 garlic clove, crushed
2 x 400g/14oz cans chopped tomatoes
15ml/1 tbsp tomato purée
4 black olives, stoned and chopped
5ml/1 tsp dried thyme

1 Preheat the oven to 190°C/375°F/Gas 5 and lightly grease an ovenproof dish with olive oil. Bring a large saucepan of water to the boil, add a little olive oil and simmer the cannelloni tubes, uncovered, for about 6–7 minutes, or until nearly cooked.

2 Meanwhile, steam or boil the broccoli for 10 minutes, until tender. Drain the pasta, rinse under cold water and reserve. Drain the broccoli and leave to cool, then place in a blender or food processor and process until smooth. Set aside.

3 Place the breadcrumbs in a bowl, add the milk and oil and stir until softened. Add the ricotta, broccoli purée, nutmeg, 60ml/4 tbsp of the Parmesan cheese and seasoning, then set aside.

4 To make the sauce, heat the oil in a frying pan; add the onion and garlic. Fry for 5–6 minutes, until softened, then stir in the tomatoes, tomato purée, black olives, thyme and seasoning. Boil rapidly for 2–3 minutes, then pour into the base of the dish.

5 Spoon the cheese mixture into a piping bag fitted with a 1cm/½in nozzle. Carefully open the cannelloni tubes. Standing each one upright on a board, pipe the filling into each tube. Lay them in rows in the tomato sauce.

6 Brush the tops of the cannelloni with a little olive oil and sprinkle over the remaining Parmesan cheese and pine nuts. Bake for about 25–30 minutes, until golden on top.

Baked Tortellini with Three Cheeses

Serve this straight out of the oven while the cheese is still runny. If smoked mozzarella cheese is not available, try using a smoked German cheese or even grated smoked Cheddar.

INGREDIENTS

Serves 4–6

450g/1lb fresh tortellini
2 eggs
350g/12oz/1½ cups ricotta or curd cheese
25g/1oz/2 tbsp butter
25g/1oz fresh basil leaves
115g/4oz smoked mozzarella cheese
60ml/4 tbsp freshly grated Parmesan cheese
salt and ground black pepper

1 Preheat the oven to 190°C/375°F/Gas 5. Cook the fresh tortellini in plenty of boiling salted water according to the instructions on the packet. Drain well.

2 Beat the eggs with the ricotta or curd cheese and season well with salt and pepper. Use the butter to grease an ovenproof dish. Spoon in half the tortellini, pour over half the cheese mixture and cover with half the basil leaves.

3 Cover with the mozzarella and remaining basil. Top with the rest of the tortellini and spread over the remaining ricotta or curd cheese mixture.

4 Sprinkle evenly with the Parmesan cheese. Bake in the oven for 35–45 minutes or until golden brown and bubbling.

Cannelloni

This version of a classic Italian dish introduces a variety of vegetables which are topped with a traditional cheese sauce.

INGREDIENTS

Serves 4

8 cannelloni tubes
115g/4oz spinach

For the filling

15ml/1 tbsp oil
175g/6oz/1½ cups minced beef
2 garlic cloves, crushed
25g/1oz/2 tbsp plain flour
120ml/4fl oz/½ cup beef stock
1 small carrot, finely chopped
1 small yellow courgette, chopped
salt and ground black pepper

For the sauce

25g/1oz/2 tbsp butter
25g/1oz/2 tbsp plain flour
250ml/8fl oz/1 cup milk
50g/2oz/½ cup freshly grated Parmesan cheese

1 Preheat the oven to 180°C/350°F/Gas 4. For the filling, heat the oil in a large pan. Add the minced beef and garlic. Cook for 5 minutes.

2 Add the flour and cook for a further 1 minute. Slowly stir in the stock and bring to the boil.

3 Add the carrot and courgette. Season. Cook for 10 minutes.

4 Spoon the mince mixture into the cannelloni tubes and place in an ovenproof dish.

5 Blanch the spinach in boiling water for 3 minutes. Drain well and place on top of the cannelloni tubes in the dish.

6 For the sauce melt the butter in a pan. Add the flour and cook for 1 minute. Pour in the milk, add the grated cheese and season well. Bring to the boil, stirring all the time. Pour over the cannelloni and spinach and bake for 30 minutes. Serve with tomatoes and a crisp green salad, if liked.

Pasta Spirals with Lentils and Cheese

This surprising combination works extremely well.

INGREDIENTS

Serves 4

15ml/1 tbsp olive oil
1 onion, chopped
1 garlic clove, chopped
1 carrot, cut into matchsticks
350g/12oz pasta spirals, such as fusilli
65g/2½oz/½ cup green lentils, boiled for 25 minutes
15ml/1 tbsp tomato purée
15ml/1 tbsp chopped fresh oregano
150ml/¼ pint/⅔ cup vegetable stock
225g/8oz/2 cups grated Cheddar cheese
salt and ground black pepper
freshly grated cheese, to serve

1 Heat the oil in a large frying pan and fry the onion and garlic for 3 minutes. Add the carrot and cook for a further 5 minutes.

COOK'S TIP

Tomato purée is sold in small cans and tubes. If you use a can for this small amount, you can keep the remainder fresh by transferring it to a bowl, covering it with a thin layer of olive oil and putting it in the fridge until needed.

2 Cook the pasta in plenty of boiling salted water according to the instructions on the packet.

3 Add the lentils, tomato purée and oregano to the frying pan, stir, cover and cook for 3 minutes.

4 Add the stock and salt and pepper to the pan. Cover and simmer for 10 minutes. Add the grated Cheddar cheese.

5 Drain the pasta thoroughly and stir into the sauce to coat. Serve with plenty of extra grated cheese.

Pasta Spirals with Chicken and Tomato

A recipe for a speedy supper – serve this dish with a mixed bean salad.

INGREDIENTS

Serves 4

15ml/1 tbsp olive oil
1 onion, chopped
1 carrot, chopped
50g/2oz sun-dried tomatoes in olive oil, drained weight
1 garlic clove, chopped
400g/14oz can chopped tomatoes, drained
15ml/1 tbsp tomato purée
150ml/¼ pint/⅔ cup chicken stock
350g/12oz fusilli
225g/8oz chicken, diagonally sliced
salt and ground black pepper
fresh mint sprigs, to garnish

1 Heat the oil in a large frying pan and fry the onion and carrot for 5 minutes, stirring the vegetables occasionally.

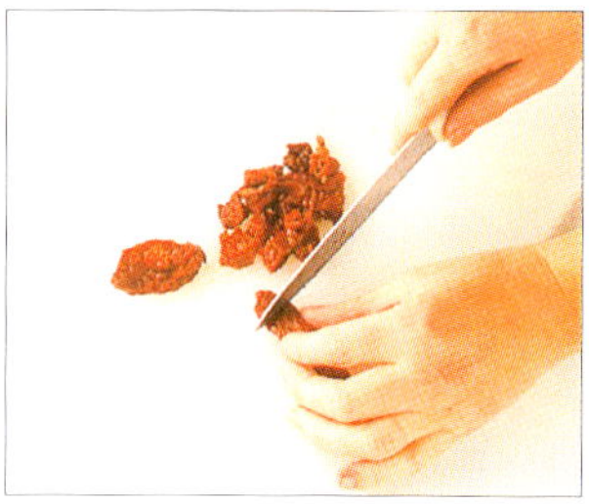

2 Chop the sun-dried tomatoes and set aside until needed.

3 Stir the garlic, tomatoes, tomato purée and stock into the onions and carrots and bring to the boil. Simmer for 10 minutes, stirring occasionally.

4 Cook the pasta in plenty of boiling salted water according to the instructions on the packet.

5 Pour the sauce into a blender or food processor and process until smooth.

6 Return the sauce to the pan and stir in the sun-dried tomatoes and chicken. Bring back to the boil and then simmer for 10 minutes until the chicken is cooked. Adjust the seasoning, if necessary.

7 Drain the pasta thoroughly and toss in the sauce. Serve at once, garnished with sprigs of fresh mint.

Lasagne al Forno

The classic version of this dish is pasta layered with meat sauce and creamy béchamel sauce. You could vary it by using mozzarella cheese instead of the béchamel sauce, or by mixing ricotta cheese, Parmesan and herbs together instead of the traditional meat sauce.

INGREDIENTS

Serves 4–6

about 12 sheets dried lasagne
1 quantity Bolognese Sauce
about 50g/2oz/½ cup freshly grated Parmesan cheese
tomato slices and parsley sprig, to garnish

For the béchamel sauce

900ml/1½ pints/3¾ cups milk
sliced onion, carrot and celery
a few whole black peppercorns
50g/2oz/½ cup butter
75g/3oz/¾ cup plain flour
freshly grated nutmeg
salt and ground black pepper

1 First make the béchamel sauce. Pour the milk into a saucepan and add the vegetables and peppercorns. Bring to boiling point, remove from the heat and leave to infuse for at least 30 minutes.

2 Strain the milk into a jug. Then melt the butter in the same saucepan and stir in the flour. Cook, stirring, for 2 minutes.

3 Remove from the heat and add the milk all at once, whisk well and return to the heat. Bring to the boil, whisking all the time, then simmer for 2–3 minutes, stirring constantly until thickened. Season to taste with nutmeg, salt and ground black pepper.

4 Preheat the oven to 180°C/350°F/Gas 4. If necessary, cook the sheets of lasagne in plenty of boiling salted water according to the instructions on the packet. Lift out with a slotted spoon and drain on a clean dish towel. Spoon a third of the meat sauce into a buttered baking-dish.

5 Place four sheets of lasagne over the meat sauce. Spread with one-third of the béchamel sauce. Repeat twice more, finishing with a layer of béchamel sauce covering the whole top.

6 Sprinkle with Parmesan cheese and bake in the oven for about 45 minutes until brown. Serve garnished with tomato slices and a sprig of parsley.

Baked Lasagne with Meat Sauce

This lasagne made from egg pasta with homemade meat and béchamel sauce is exquisite.

INGREDIENTS

Serves 8–10

2 quantities Bolognese Meat Sauce

egg pasta sheets made with 3 eggs or 400g/14oz dried lasagne

115g/4oz/1 cup grated Parmesan cheese

40g/1½oz/3 tbsp butter

For the béchamel sauce

750ml/1¼ pints/3 cups milk

1 bay leaf

3 mace blades

115g/4oz/½ cup butter

75g/3oz/¾ cup plain flour

salt and ground black pepper

1 Prepare the meat sauce and set aside. Butter a large shallow baking dish, preferably rectangular or square.

COOK'S TIP

If you are using dried or bought pasta, follow step 4, but boil the lasagne in just two batches, and stop the cooking about 4 minutes before the recommended cooking time on the packet has elapsed. Rinse in cold water and lay the pasta out the same way as for the egg pasta.

2 Make the béchamel sauce by gently heating the milk with the bay leaf and mace in a small saucepan. Melt the butter in a medium heavy-based saucepan. Add the flour, and mix well with a wire whisk. Cook for 2–3 minutes. Strain the hot milk into the flour and butter, and mix smoothly with the whisk. Bring the sauce to the boil, stirring constantly, and cook for a further 4–5 minutes. Season with salt and pepper and set aside.

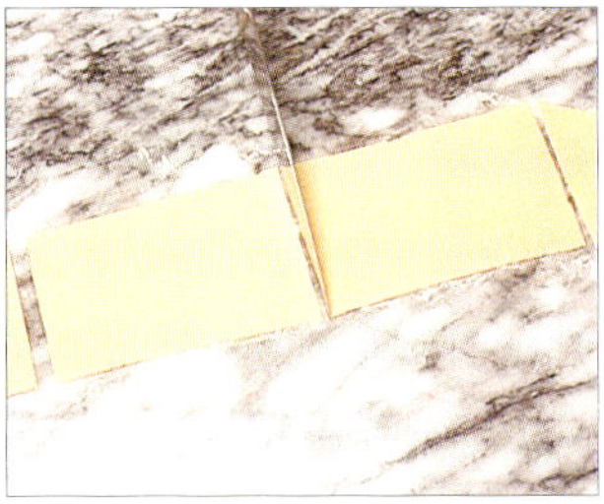

3 Make the pasta. Do not let it dry out before cutting it into rectangles measuring about 11cm/4½in wide and the same length as the baking dish (this will make it easier to assemble later). Preheat the oven to 200°C/400°F/Gas 6.

4 Bring a very large pan of water to the boil. Place a large bowl of cold water near the cooker. Cover a large work surface with a tablecloth. Add salt to the rapidly boiling water. Drop in 3 or 4 of the egg pasta rectangles. Cook very briefly, about 30 seconds. Remove from the pan, using a slotted spoon, and drop into the cold water for about 30 seconds. Pull them out of the water, shaking off the excess water. Lay them out flat without overlapping on the tablecloth. Continue with all the remaining pasta and trimmings.

5 To assemble the lasagne, spread one large spoonful of the meat sauce over the base of the dish. Arrange a layer of pasta in the dish, cutting it with a sharp knife so that it fits well.

6 Cover with a thin layer of meat sauce, then one of béchamel. Sprinkle with a little cheese. Repeat the layers in the same order, and ending with a layer of pasta coated with béchamel. Do not make more than about 6 layers of pasta. Use the pasta trimmings to patch any gaps in the pasta. Sprinkle the top with grated Parmesan cheese, and dot with butter.

7 Bake in the preheated oven for 20 minutes, or until brown on top. Remove from the oven and allow to stand for about 5 minutes before serving. Serve directly from the baking dish, cutting out rectangular or square sections for each helping.

Leek and Chèvre Lasagne

An unusual and lighter than average lasagne using a soft French goat's cheese. The pasta sheets are not so chewy if boiled briefly first, or you could use no-precook lasagne instead if you prefer.

INGREDIENTS

Serves 6

6–8 lasagne sheets
1 large aubergine, sliced
3 leeks, thinly sliced
30ml/2 tbsp olive oil
2 red peppers, roasted
200g/7oz chèvre, broken into pieces
50g/2oz/½ cup freshly grated pecorino or Parmesan cheese

For the sauce

65g/2½oz/9 tbsp plain flour
65g/2½oz/5 tbsp butter
900ml/1½ pints/3¾ cups milk
2.5ml/½ tsp ground bay leaves
freshly grated nutmeg
salt and ground black pepper

1 Blanch the pasta sheets in plenty of boiling water for just 2 minutes. Drain and place on a clean dish towel.

2 Lightly salt the aubergine slices and place in a colander to drain for 30 minutes, then rinse and pat dry with kitchen paper.

3 Preheat the oven to 190°C/375°F/Gas 5. Lightly fry the leeks in the oil for 5 minutes, until softened. Peel the roasted peppers and cut into strips.

4 To make the sauce, put the flour, butter and milk into a saucepan and bring to the boil, stirring constantly until thickened. Add the ground bay leaves, nutmeg and seasoning. Simmer the sauce for a further 2 minutes.

5 In a greased shallow casserole, layer the leeks, lasagne sheets, aubergine, chèvre and pecorino or Parmesan. Trickle the sauce over the layers, ensuring that plenty goes in-between.

6 Finish with a layer of sauce and grated cheese. Bake in the oven for 30 minutes, or until bubbling and browned on top. Serve immediately.

Macaroni and Blue Cheese

The blue cheese gives this simple dish a new twist.

INGREDIENTS

Serves 6

450g/1lb macaroni
900ml/1½ pints/3¾ cups milk
50g/2oz/4 tbsp butter
75g/3oz/6 tbsp plain flour
1.5ml/¼ tsp salt
225g/8oz blue cheese, crumbled
ground black pepper

1 Preheat the oven to 180°C/350°F/Gas 4. Lightly grease a 33 × 23cm/12 × 9in baking dish.

2 Cook the macaroni in plenty of boiling salted water according to the instructions on the packet, or until *al dente*. Drain and rinse under cold water. Place in a large bowl and set aside.

3 In another pan, bring the milk to the boil and set aside.

4 Melt the butter in a heavy-based saucepan over a low heat. Whisk in the flour and cook for 5 minutes, whisking continuously. Be careful not to let the mixture brown.

5 Remove from the heat and whisk the hot milk into the butter and flour mixture. When smoothly blended, return to a medium heat and continue cooking for about 5 minutes, whisking constantly until the sauce is thick. Add the salt.

6 Add the sauce to the macaroni. Add three-quarters of the crumbled blue cheese and stir well. Transfer the macaroni mixture to the prepared baking dish and spread in an even layer.

7 Sprinkle the remaining cheese evenly over the surface. Bake for 25 minutes, until bubbling hot.

8 If desired, lightly brown the top of the macaroni and cheese under the grill for 3–4 minutes. Serve hot, sprinkled with ground black pepper to taste.

QUICK & EASY

Linguine with Pesto Sauce

Pesto originates in Liguria, where the sea breezes are said to give the local basil a particularly fine flavour. It is traditionally made with a pestle and mortar, but it is easier to make in a food processor or blender. Freeze any spare pesto in an ice-cube tray for later use.

INGREDIENTS

Serves 5–6

65g/2½oz/¾ cup fresh basil leaves
3–4 cloves garlic, peeled
45ml/3 tbsp pine nuts
2.5ml/½ tsp salt
75ml/5 tbsp olive oil
50g/2oz/½ cup freshly grated Parmesan cheese
60ml/4 tbsp freshly grated pecorino cheese
ground black pepper
500g/1¼lb linguine

1 Place the basil, garlic, pine nuts, salt and olive oil in a blender or food processor and process until smooth. Remove to a bowl. If desired, the sauce may be frozen at this point, before the cheeses are added.

2 Stir in the cheeses (use all Parmesan if pecorino is not available). Taste for seasoning.

3 Cook the pasta in a large pan of rapidly boiling salted water until it is *al dente*. Just before draining, take about 60ml/4 tbsp of the cooking water and stir into the pesto sauce.

4 Drain the pasta thoroughly and toss it together with the sauce. Serve immediately.

Pappardelle, with Beans and Mushrooms

A mixture of wild and cultivated mushrooms help to give this dish a rich and nutty flavour.

INGREDIENTS

Serves 4

30ml/2 tbsp olive oil
50g/2oz/4 tbsp butter
2 shallots, chopped
2–3 garlic cloves, crushed
675g/1½lb mixed mushrooms, thickly sliced
4 sun-dried tomatoes in oil, drained and chopped
90ml/6 tbsp dry white wine
400g/14oz can borlotti beans, drained
45ml/3 tbsp grated Parmesan cheese
chopped fresh parsley, to garnish
salt and ground black pepper
cooked pappardelle, to serve

1 Heat the oil and butter in a frying pan and fry the shallots until they are soft.

2 Add the garlic and mushrooms and fry for 3–4 minutes. Stir in the sun-dried tomatoes, wine and add seasoning to taste.

3 Stir in the borlotti beans and cook for 5–6 minutes, until most of the liquid has evaporated from the pan and the beans are warmed through.

4 Stir in the grated Parmesan cheese. Sprinkle with parsley and serve immediately with freshly cooked pappardelle.

Orecchiette with Broccoli

Puglia, in southern Italy, specializes in imaginative pasta and vegetable combinations. Using the broccoli cooking water for boiling the pasta gives it more of the vegetable's lovely fresh flavour.

INGREDIENTS

Serves 6

800g/1¾lb broccoli
450g/1lb orecchiette or penne
90ml/6 tbsp olive oil
3 garlic cloves, finely chopped
6 anchovy fillets in oil
salt and ground black pepper

1 Peel the stems of the broccoli, starting from the base and pulling up towards the florets with a knife. Discard the woody parts of the stem. Cut the florets and stems into 5cm/2in pieces.

2 Bring a large pan of water to the boil. Drop in the broccoli and boil until barely tender, about 5–8 minutes. Remove the broccoli pieces from the pan to a serving bowl. Do not discard the broccoli cooking water.

3 Add salt to the broccoli cooking water and bring back to the boil. Drop in the pasta, stir well, and cook until *al dente*.

4 While the pasta is boiling, heat the oil in a small saucepan. Add the garlic and, after 2–3 minutes, the anchovy fillets. Using a fork, mash the anchovies and garlic to a smooth paste. Then cook for a further 3–4 minutes.

5 Before draining the pasta, ladle 1–2 cupfuls of the cooking water over the broccoli. Add the drained pasta and the hot anchovy and oil mixture. Mix well, and season with salt and pepper if necessary. Serve at once.

Spaghetti with Eggs and Bacon

One of the classic pasta sauces, about which a debate still remains: whether or not it should contain cream. Pasta purists believe that it should not.

INGREDIENTS

Serves 4

30ml/2 tbsp olive oil
150g/5oz bacon, cut into matchsticks
1 garlic clove, crushed
400g/14oz spaghetti
3 eggs, at room temperature
75g/3oz/¾ cup freshly grated Parmesan cheese
salt and ground black pepper

1 In a medium frying pan, heat the oil and sauté the bacon and the garlic until the bacon renders its fat and starts to brown. Remove and discard the garlic. Keep the bacon and its fat hot, until needed.

2 Cook the spaghetti in plenty of rapidly boiling salted water until *al dente*.

3 Meanwhile, warm a large serving bowl and break the eggs into it. Beat in the Parmesan cheese with a fork, and season with salt and pepper.

4 As soon as the pasta is done, drain it quickly, and mix it into the egg mixture. Pour on the hot bacon and its fat. Stir well. The heat from the pasta and bacon fat will lightly cook the beaten eggs. Serve immediately.

Rigatoni with Garlic Crumbs

A hot and spicy dish – halve the quantity of chilli if you like a milder flavour. The bacon is an optional addition; you can leave it out if you are cooking for vegetarians.

INGREDIENTS

Serves 4–6

45ml/3 tbsp olive oil
2 shallots, chopped
8 rashers streaky bacon, chopped (optional)
10ml/2 tsp crushed dried red chillies
400g/14oz can chopped tomatoes with garlic and herbs
6 slices white bread
115g/4oz/½ cup butter
2 garlic cloves, chopped
450g/1lb rigatoni
salt and ground black pepper

1 Heat the oil in a medium saucepan and fry the shallots and bacon, if using, gently for 6–8 minutes until golden. Add the dried chillies and chopped tomatoes, half-cover and simmer for 20 minutes.

2 Meanwhile, cut the crusts off the bread and discard them. Reduce the bread to crumbs in a blender or food processor.

3 Heat the butter in a frying pan, add the garlic and bread-crumbs and stir-fry until golden and crisp. (Don't let the crumbs catch and burn or the final result will be ruined.)

4 Cook the pasta in plenty of boiling salted water according to the instructions on the packet, until *al dente*. Drain well.

5 Toss the pasta with the tomato sauce and divide among four or six warmed serving plates.

6 Sprinkle with the crumbs and serve immediately.

Paglia e Fieno

The title of this dish translates as "straw and hay" which refers to the yellow and green colours of the pasta when mixed together. Fresh peas make all the difference to this dish.

INGREDIENTS

Serves 4

50g/2oz/4 tbsp butter
350g/12oz/3 cups frozen petits pois or 900g/2lb fresh peas, shelled
150ml/¼ pint/⅔ cup double cream, plus 60ml/4 tbsp extra
450g/1lb tagliatelle (plain and green mixed)
50g/2oz/½ cup freshly grated Parmesan cheese, plus extra to serve
freshly grated nutmeg
salt and ground black pepper

1 Melt the butter in a heavy saucepan and add the peas. Sauté for 2–3 minutes, then add the cream, bring to the boil and simmer for 1 minute until the mixture is slightly thickened.

2 Cook the plain and green mixed tagliatelle in plenty of boiling salted water according to the instructions on the packet, but for 2 minutes less time, until it is just *al dente*. Drain well and then turn into the saucepan containing the cream and pea sauce.

3 Place on the heat and turn the pasta in the sauce to coat. Pour in the extra cream, the cheese, salt and pepper to taste and a little grated nutmeg. Toss until well coated and heated through. Serve immediately with extra freshly grated Parmesan cheese.

COOK'S TIP

Sautéed mushrooms and narrow strips of cooked ham also make good additions to this dish.

Pasta Napoletana

The simple classic cooked tomato sauce with no adornments.

INGREDIENTS

Serves 4

900g/2lb fresh ripe red tomatoes or 750g/1¾lb canned plum tomatoes with their juice
1 onion, chopped
1 carrot, diced
1 celery stick, diced
150ml/¼ pint/⅔ cup dry white wine (optional)
1 sprig fresh parsley
pinch of caster sugar
15ml/1 tbsp chopped fresh oregano or 5ml/1 tsp dried
450g/1lb pasta, any variety
salt and ground black pepper
freshly grated Parmesan cheese, to serve

1 Roughly chop the tomatoes and place in a medium saucepan.

2 Add all the other ingredients, except the oregano, pasta and cheese, and bring to the boil. Simmer, half-covered, for about 45 minutes until very thick, stirring occasionally. Strain, then stir in the oregano. Taste and adjust the seasoning if necessary.

3 Cook the pasta in plenty of boiling salted water according to the instructions on the packet, until *al dente*. Drain well.

4 Toss the pasta with the sauce. Serve with plenty of freshly grated Parmesan cheese.

Mushroom and Chilli Carbonara

For a richer mushroom flavour, use a small packet of dried Italian porcini mushrooms in this quick eggy sauce, and for an extra spicy zing, toss in some chilli flakes too.

INGREDIENTS

Serves 4

15g/½oz pack dried porcini mushrooms
300ml/½ pint/1¼ cups hot water
225g/8oz spaghetti
1 garlic clove, crushed
25g/1oz/2 tbsp butter
15ml/1 tbsp olive oil
225g/8oz button or chestnut mushrooms, thinly sliced
5ml/1 tsp dried red chilli flakes
2 eggs
300ml/½ pint/1¼ cups single cream
salt and ground black pepper
freshly grated Parmesan cheese and chopped fresh parsley, to serve

1 Soak the dried mushrooms in the hot water for 15 minutes; drain and reserve the liquor.

2 Cook the spaghetti according to the instructions in plenty of boiling salted water. Drain and rinse in cold water.

3 In a large saucepan, lightly sauté the garlic with the butter and oil for half a minute.

4 Add the mushrooms, including the soaked porcini ones, and the chilli flakes, and stir well. Cook for about 2 minutes.

5 Pour in the reserved soaking liquor from the mushrooms and boil the mixture to reduce slightly.

6 Beat the eggs with the cream and season well. Return the cooked spaghetti to the pan and toss in the eggs and cream. Reheat, without boiling, and serve hot sprinkled with grated Parmesan cheese and chopped parsley.

VARIATION

Instead of mushrooms, try using either finely sliced and sautéed leeks or perhaps coarsely shredded lettuce with peas. If chilli flakes are too hot and spicy for you, then try the delicious alternative of skinned and chopped tomatoes with torn, fresh basil leaves.

Tagliatelle with "Hit-the-pan" Salsa

It is possible to make a hot, filling meal within just 15 minutes with this quick-cook salsa sauce. If you have no time don't peel the tomatoes.

INGREDIENTS

Serves 2

115g/4oz tagliatelle
45ml/3 tbsp olive oil, preferably extra virgin
3 large tomatoes
1 garlic clove, crushed
4 spring onions, sliced
1 green chilli, halved, seeded and sliced
juice of 1 orange (optional)
30ml/2 tbsp chopped fresh parsley
salt and ground black pepper
grated cheese, to serve (optional)

1 Cook the tagliatelle in plenty of boiling salted water until *al dente*. Drain and toss in a little of the oil. Season well.

2 Skin the tomatoes by dipping them in a bowl of boiling water for about 45 seconds and then into cold water. The skins should slip off easily. Roughly chop the flesh.

3 Heat the remaining oil until quite hot and stir-fry the garlic, onions and chilli for 1 minute.

4 Add the tomatoes, orange juice, if using, and parsley. Season well and stir in the tagliatelle to reheat. Serve with grated cheese, if desired.

COOK'S TIP

You could use any pasta shape for this recipe. It would be particularly good with large rigatoni or linguini, or as a sauce for fresh ravioli or tortellini.

Spaghetti with Garlic and Oil

This is one of the simplest and most satisfying pasta dishes of all. It is very popular throughout Italy. Use the best quality oil available for this splendid dish.

INGREDIENTS

Serves 4

400g/14oz spaghetti
90ml/6 tbsp extra virgin olive oil
3 garlic cloves, chopped
60ml/4 tbsp chopped fresh parsley
salt and ground black pepper
freshly grated Parmesan cheese, to serve (optional)

1 Cook the spaghetti in plenty of boiling salted water.

2 In a large frying pan heat the oil and gently sauté the garlic until barely golden. Do not let it brown or it will taste bitter. Stir in the chopped fresh parsley, then season with salt and pepper. Remove from the heat until the pasta is ready.

3 Drain the pasta when it is barely *al dente*. Tip it into the pan with the oil and garlic, and cook together for 2–3 minutes, stirring well to coat the spaghetti with the sauce. Serve at once in a warmed serving bowl, with some Parmesan cheese, if desired.

Spaghetti with Walnut Sauce

Like pesto, this sauce is traditionally ground in a pestle and mortar , but works just as well made in a blender or food processor. It is also good on tagliatelle and other pasta noodles.

INGREDIENTS

Serves 4

115g/4oz/1 cup walnut pieces or halves
45ml/3 tbsp plain breadcrumbs
45ml/3 tbsp olive or walnut oil
45ml/3 tbsp chopped fresh parsley
1–2 garlic cloves (optional)
50g/2oz/¼ cup butter, at room temperature
30ml/2 tbsp double cream
400g/14oz wholemeal spaghetti
salt and ground black pepper
freshly grated Parmesan cheese, to serve

1 Drop the nuts into a small pan of boiling water, and cook for 1–2 minutes. Drain, then skin. Dry on kitchen paper. Coarsely chop and set aside about a quarter.

2 Place the remaining nuts, the breadcrumbs, oil, parsley and garlic, if using, in a blender or food processor. Process to a paste. Remove to a bowl, and stir in the softened butter and the cream. Season with salt and pepper.

3 Cook the pasta in plenty of boiling salted water, following the instructions on the packet, until *al dente*. Drain, then toss with the sauce. Sprinkle with the reserved chopped nuts, and hand round the grated Parmesan separately.

Campanelle with Yellow Pepper Sauce

Roasted yellow peppers make a deliciously sweet and creamy sauce to serve with pasta.

INGREDIENTS

Serves 4

2 yellow peppers
50g/2oz/¼ cup soft goat's cheese
115g/4oz/½ cup low-fat fromage blanc
450g/1lb short pasta, such as campanelle or fusilli
salt and ground black pepper
50g/2oz/½ cup toasted flaked almonds, to serve

1 Place the whole yellow peppers under a preheated grill until charred and blistered. Place in a plastic bag, seal and leave to cool. Then peel and remove all the seeds.

2 Place the pepper flesh in a blender or food processor with the goat's cheese and fromage blanc. Process until smooth. Season with salt and plenty of ground black pepper.

3 Cook the pasta in plenty of boiling salted water, according to the instructions on the packet, until *al dente*. Drain well.

4 Toss with the sauce and serve sprinkled with the toasted flaked almonds.

Spaghetti with Olives and Mushrooms

A rich, pungent sauce topped with sweet cherry tomatoes.

INGREDIENTS

Serves 4

- 15ml/1 tbsp olive oil
- 1 garlic clove, chopped
- 225g/8oz mushrooms, chopped
- 150g/5oz/scant 1 cup black olives, stoned
- 30ml/2 tbsp chopped fresh parsley
- 1 red chilli, seeded and chopped
- 450g/1lb spaghetti
- 225g/8oz cherry tomatoes
- Parmesan cheese shavings, to serve (optional)

1 Heat the oil in a large pan. Add the garlic; cook for 1 minute. Add the chopped mushrooms, cover, and cook over a medium heat for 5 minutes.

2 Place the mushrooms in a blender or food processor with the olives, parsley and red chilli. Blend until smooth.

3 Cook the pasta in plenty of boiling salted water, according to the instructions on the packet, until *al dente*. Drain well and return to the pan. Add the olive mixture and toss together until the pasta is well coated. Cover and keep warm.

4 Heat an ungreased frying pan and shake the cherry tomatoes around until they start to split, about 2–3 minutes. Serve the pasta topped with the tomatoes and garnished with Parmesan cheese shavings, if desired.

Pasta with Spring Vegetables

Don't be tempted to use dried herbs in this flavoursome dish.

INGREDIENTS

Serves 4

115g/4oz broccoli florets
115g/4oz baby leeks
225g/8oz asparagus
1 small fennel bulb
115g/4oz/1 cup fresh or frozen peas
40g/1½oz/3 tbsp butter
1 shallot, chopped
45ml/3 tbsp chopped fresh mixed herbs, such as parsley, thyme and sage
300ml/½ pint/1¼ cups double cream
350g/12oz dried penne
salt and ground black pepper
freshly grated Parmesan cheese, to serve

1 Divide the broccoli florets into tiny sprigs. Cut the leeks and asparagus diagonally into 5cm/2in lengths. Trim the fennel bulb and remove any tough outer leaves. Cut into wedges, leaving the layers attached at the root ends so the pieces stay intact.

2 Cook each vegetable, including the peas, separately in boiling salted water until just tender – use the same water for each vegetable. Drain well and keep warm.

3 Melt the butter in a separate pan, add the chopped shallot and cook, stirring occasionally, until softened but not browned. Stir in the herbs and cream and cook for a few minutes, until slightly thickened.

4 Meanwhile, cook the pasta in plenty of boiling salted water for 10 minutes until *al dente*. Drain well and add to the sauce with the vegetables. Toss gently and season with plenty of pepper.

5 Serve the pasta hot with a sprinkling of freshly grated Parmesan cheese.

Tagliatelle with Spinach and Garlic Cheese

It's fun to mix ingredients from different cuisines and produce a delicious dish as a result. Italian pasta and spinach combine with Chinese soy sauce and French garlic-and-herb cream cheese to create this mouthwatering and wonderfully rich dish.

INGREDIENTS

Serves 4

225g/8oz tagliatelle, preferably mixed colours
225g/8oz fresh leaf spinach
30ml/2 tbsp light soy sauce
75g/3oz garlic-and-herb cheese
45ml/3 tbsp milk
salt and ground black pepper

1 Cook the tagliatelle in plenty of boiling salted water according to the instructions on the packet. Drain and return to the pan.

2 Blanch the spinach in a tiny amount of water until just wilted, then drain well, squeezing dry with the back of a wooden spoon. Chop roughly with scissors.

3 Return the spinach to its pan and stir in the soy sauce, garlic-and-herb cheese and milk. Bring slowly to the boil, stirring until smooth. Season to taste.

4 When the sauce is ready, pour over the pasta. Toss the pasta and sauce together and serve hot.

Spaghetti Olio e Aglio

This is a classic recipe from Rome. Originally the food of the poor, involving nothing more than pasta, olive oil (olio) and garlic (aglio), this is a quick and filling dish which is fast becoming fashionable the world over.

INGREDIENTS

Serves 4

2 garlic cloves
30ml/2 tbsp roughly chopped fresh parsley
120ml/4fl oz/½ cup olive oil
450g/1lb spaghetti
salt and ground black pepper

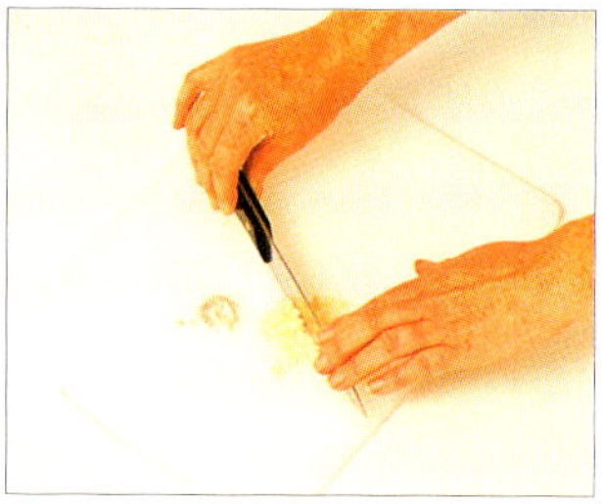

1 Using a sharp knife, peel and finely chop the two cloves of garlic.

2 Using a nylon chopping board and a sharp knife, roughly chop the fresh parsley.

3 Heat the olive oil in a medium saucepan and add the garlic and a pinch of salt. Cook gently, stirring all the time, until golden. If the garlic becomes too brown, it will taste bitter and spoil the dish.

4 Meanwhile cook the spaghetti in plenty of boiling salted water according to the instructions on the packet until *al dente*. Drain well through a colander.

5 Toss with the warm – not sizzling – garlic and oil and add plenty of black pepper and the parsley. Serve immediately.

Spaghetti with Fresh Tomato Sauce

The heat from the pasta will release the delicious flavours of this sauce. Only use the really red and soft tomatoes – large ripe beefsteak or Marmande tomatoes are ideal. Don't be tempted to use small hard tomatoes: they have very little flavour.

INGREDIENTS

Serves 4

4 large ripe tomatoes
2 garlic cloves, finely chopped
60ml/4 tbsp chopped fresh herbs, such as basil, marjoram, oregano or parsley
150ml/¼ pint/⅔ cup olive oil
450g/1lb spaghetti
salt and ground black pepper

1 Skin the tomatoes by placing in boiling water for 1 minute. Lift out with a slotted spoon and plunge into a bowl of cold water. Peel off the skins, then dry the tomatoes on kitchen paper.

2 Halve the tomatoes and squeeze out the seeds. Chop into 5mm/¼in cubes and mix with the garlic, herbs, olive oil and seasoning in a non-metallic bowl. Cover and allow the flavours to mellow for at least 30 minutes.

3 Cook the pasta in plenty of boiling salted water, according to the instructions on the packet.

4 Drain the pasta and mix with the sauce. Cover with a lid and leave for 2–3 minutes, then toss again and serve immediately.

VARIATION

Mix 115g/4oz/1 cup stoned and chopped black Greek olives into the sauce just before serving.

Tortellini with Cream, Butter and Cheese

This is an indulgent but quick alternative to macaroni cheese. Stir in some ham or pepperoni if you wish, though it's quite delicious as it is!

INGREDIENTS

Serves 4–6

450g/1lb fresh tortellini
50g/2oz/4 tbsp butter
300ml/½ pint/1¼ cups double cream
115g/4oz Parmesan cheese
freshly grated nutmeg
salt and ground black pepper

1 Cook the pasta in plenty of boiling salted water according to the instructions on the packet.

2 Meanwhile melt the butter in a medium saucepan and stir in the cream. Bring to the boil and cook for 2–3 minutes until the mixture is slightly thickened.

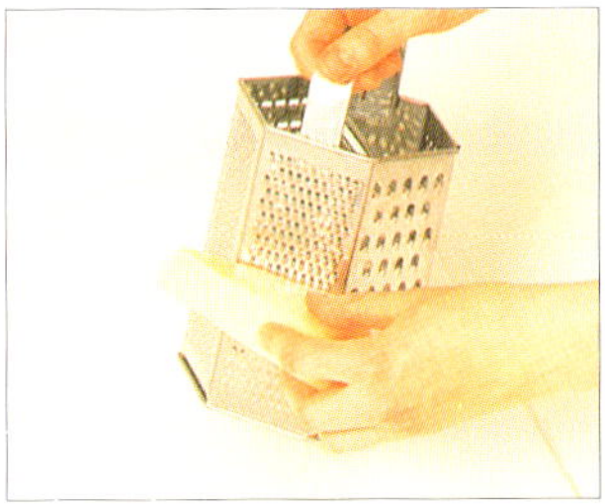

3 Grate the Parmesan cheese and stir 75g/3oz/¾ cup of it into the sauce until melted. Season to taste with salt, black pepper and nutmeg. Preheat the grill.

4 Drain the pasta well and spoon into a buttered heatproof serving dish. Pour over the sauce, sprinkle over the remaining cheese and place under the grill until brown and bubbling. Serve the tortellini immediately.

Greek Pasta with Avocado Sauce

This is an unusual sauce with a pale green colour, studded with red tomato. It has a luxurious, velvety texture. The sauce is rather rich, so you don't need too much of it.

INGREDIENTS

Serves 6

3 ripe tomatoes
2 large ripe avocados
25g/1oz/2 tbsp butter, plus extra for tossing the pasta
1 garlic clove, crushed
350ml/12fl oz/1½ cups double cream
dash of Tabasco sauce
450g/1lb green tagliatelle
salt and ground black pepper
freshly grated Parmesan cheese, to garnish
60ml/4 tbsp soured cream, to garnish

1 Halve the tomatoes and remove the cores. Squeeze out the seeds and dice the flesh. Set aside until required.

2 Halve the avocados, remove the stones and peel. Roughly chop the flesh. If hard-skinned, scoop out the flesh with a spoon.

3 Melt the butter in a saucepan and add the garlic. Cook for 1 minute, then add the cream and chopped avocados. Increase the heat, stirring constantly to break up the avocados.

4 Add the diced tomatoes and season to taste with salt, pepper and a little Tabasco sauce. Keep the mixture warm.

5 Cook the pasta in plenty of boiling salted water according to the instructions on the packet. Drain well through a colander and toss with a knob of butter.

6 Divide the pasta among four warmed bowls and spoon over the sauce. Sprinkle with grated Parmesan cheese and top with a spoonful of soured cream.

Pasta Shells with Tomatoes and Rocket

This pretty coloured pasta dish relies for its success on the salad green, rocket. Available in large supermarkets, it is a leaf easily grown in the garden or a window-box and tastes slightly peppery.

INGREDIENTS

Serves 4

450g/1lb pasta shells
450g/1lb ripe cherry tomatoes
75g/3oz fresh rocket leaves
45ml/3 tbsp olive oil
salt and ground black pepper
Parmesan cheese shavings, to serve

1 Cook the pasta in plenty of boiling salted water according to the instructions on the packet, until *al dente*. Drain well.

2 Halve the tomatoes. Trim, wash and dry the rocket leaves.

3 Heat the oil in a large saucepan, add the tomatoes and cook for barely 1 minute. The tomatoes should only just heat through and not disintegrate.

4 Add the pasta, then the rocket. Carefully stir to mix and heat through. Season well with salt and ground black pepper. Serve immediately with plenty of Parmesan cheese shavings.

Fettuccine all'Alfredo

A classic dish from Rome, Fettuccine all'Alfredo is simply pasta tossed with double cream, butter and freshly grated Parmesan cheese. Popular additions are peas and strips of ham.

INGREDIENTS

Serves 4

25g/1oz/2 tbsp butter
150ml/¼ pint/⅔ cup double cream, plus 60ml/4 tbsp extra
450g/1lb fettuccine
50g/2oz/½ cup freshly grated Parmesan cheese, plus extra to serve
freshly grated nutmeg
salt and ground black pepper

1 Place the butter and 150ml/¼ pint/⅔ cup of the cream in a heavy saucepan, bring to the boil and simmer for 1 minute until slightly thickened.

2 Cook the fettuccine in plenty of boiling salted water according to the instructions on the packet, but for 2 minutes less time, until *al dente.*

3 Drain very well and turn into the pan with the cream sauce.

4 Place on the heat and turn the pasta in the sauce to coat thoroughly.

5 Add the extra 60ml/4 tbsp cream, the cheese, salt and pepper to taste and a little grated nutmeg. Toss until well coated and heated through. Serve at once with extra grated Parmesan cheese.

Linguine with Sweet Pepper and Cream

The sweetness of red onion complements the peppers in this dish.

INGREDIENTS

Serves 4

1 orange pepper, cored, seeded and cubed
1 yellow pepper, cored, seeded and cubed
1 red pepper, cored, seeded and cubed
350g/12oz linguine
30ml/2 tbsp olive oil
1 red onion, sliced
1 garlic clove, chopped
30ml/2 tbsp chopped fresh rosemary
150ml/¼ pint/⅔ cup double cream
salt and ground black pepper
fresh rosemary sprigs, to garnish

1 Preheat the grill to hot. Place the peppers, skin-side up, on a grill rack. Grill for 5–10 minutes until the skins begin to blister and char, turning occasionally.

2 Remove the peppers from the heat, cover with a clean dish towel and leave to stand for about 5 minutes.

3 Carefully peel away the skins from the peppers and discard. Slice the peppers into thin strips.

4 Cook the pasta in plenty of boiling salted water according to the instructions on the packet.

5 Heat the oil in a frying pan and fry the onion and garlic for about 5 minutes until softened.

6 Stir in the sliced peppers and chopped rosemary and fry gently for about 5 minutes until heated through.

7 Stir in the cream and heat through gently. Season to taste with salt and pepper.

8 Drain the pasta thoroughly and toss in the sauce. Serve immediately, garnished with sprigs of fresh rosemary.

Piquant Chicken with Spaghetti

The addition of cucumber and tomatoes adds a deliciously fresh flavour to this unusual dish.

INGREDIENTS

Serves 4

1 onion, finely chopped
1 carrot, diced
1 garlic clove, crushed
300ml/½ pint/1¼ cups vegetable stock
4 chicken breasts, boned and skinned
1 bouquet garni
115g/4oz button mushrooms, thinly sliced
5ml/1 tsp wine vinegar or lemon juice
350g/12oz spaghetti
½ cucumber, peeled and cut into fingers
2 tomatoes, skinned, seeded and chopped
30ml/2 tbsp crème fraîche
15ml/1 tbsp chopped fresh parsley
15ml/1 tbsp snipped chives
salt and ground black pepper

1 Put the onion, carrot, garlic, stock, chicken and bouquet garni into a saucepan.

2 Bring to the boil, cover and simmer for 15–20 minutes or until the chicken is tender. Transfer the chicken to a plate and cover with foil.

3 Remove the chicken and strain the liquid. Discard the vegetables and return the liquid to the pan. Add the sliced mushrooms, wine vinegar or lemon juice and simmer for 2–3 minutes.

4 Cook the spaghetti in plenty of boiling salted water according to the instructions on the packet. Drain thoroughly.

5 Blanch the cucumber in boiling water for 10 seconds. Drain and rinse under cold water.

6 Cut the chicken breasts into bite-size pieces. Boil the stock to reduce by half, then add the chicken, tomatoes, crème fraîche, cucumber and herbs. Season with salt and pepper to taste.

7 Transfer the spaghetti to a warmed serving dish and spoon over the piquant chicken. Serve at once.

Pasta Twists with Mushroom and Chorizo

The delicious combination of wild mushrooms and spicy sausage make this a tempting supper dish.

INGREDIENTS

Serves 4

350g/12oz pasta twists, such as cavatappi
60ml/4 tbsp olive oil
1 garlic clove, chopped
1 celery stick, chopped
225g/8oz chorizo sausage, sliced
225g/8oz mixed mushrooms, such as oyster, brown cap and shiitake
15ml/1 tbsp lemon juice
30ml/2 tbsp chopped fresh oregano
salt and ground black pepper
finely chopped fresh parsley, to garnish

1 Cook the pasta in plenty of boiling salted water according to the instructions on the packet.

2 Heat the oil in a frying pan and cook the garlic and celery for 5 minutes until the celery is softened but not browned.

3 Add the chorizo and cook for 5 minutes, stirring from time to time, until browned.

4 Add the mushrooms and cook for a further 4 minutes, stirring from time to time, until they are slightly softened.

5 Stir in the remaining ingredients, and heat through.

6 Drain the pasta thoroughly and turn into a serving dish. Toss with the sauce to coat. Serve immediately, garnished with finely chopped fresh parsley.

COOK'S TIP

This dish is delicious served with lashings of Parmesan cheese shavings. Use any combination of mushrooms for this flavoursome sauce.

Penne with Chicken and Ham Sauce

A meal in itself, this colourful pasta sauce is perfect for lunch or supper.

INGREDIENTS

Serves 4

350g/12oz penne
25g/1oz/2 tbsp butter
1 onion, chopped
1 garlic clove, chopped
1 bay leaf
450ml/¾ pint/1¾ cups dry white wine
150ml/¼ pint/⅔ cup crème fraîche
225g/8oz cooked chicken, skinned, boned and diced
115g/4oz cooked lean ham, diced
115g/4oz Gouda cheese, grated
15ml/1 tbsp chopped fresh mint
salt and ground black pepper
finely shredded fresh mint, to garnish

1 Cook the pasta in plenty of boiling salted water according to the instructions on the packet.

2 Heat the butter in a large frying pan and fry the onion for about 10 minutes, or until softened.

3 Add the garlic, bay leaf and wine and bring to the boil. Boil rapidly until reduced by about half. Remove the bay leaf, then stir in the crème fraîche and return to the boil.

4 Add the chicken, ham and Gouda cheese and simmer for 5 minutes, stirring occasionally until heated through.

5 Add the chopped fresh mint and season to taste.

6 Drain the pasta thoroughly and turn it into a large serving dish. Toss with the sauce, garnish with finely shredded fresh mint and serve immediately.

Tagliatelle with Peas, Asparagus and Beans

A creamy pea sauce makes a wonderful combination with crunchy young vegetables.

INGREDIENTS

Serves 4

15ml/1 tbsp olive oil
1 garlic clove, crushed
6 spring onions, sliced
225g/8oz/2 cups frozen peas, thawed
350g/12oz fresh young asparagus
30ml/2 tbsp chopped fresh sage, plus extra leaves to garnish
finely grated rind of 2 lemons
450ml/¾ pint/1¾ cups vegetable stock or water
225g/8oz/2 cups frozen broad beans, thawed
450g/1lb tagliatelle
60ml/4 tbsp low-fat natural yogurt

1 Heat the oil in a pan. Add the garlic and spring onions and cook gently for 2–3 minutes.

2 Add the peas and 115g/4oz of the asparagus, together with the sage, lemon rind and stock or water. Bring to the boil, reduce the heat and simmer for 10 minutes until tender. Purée in a blender or food processor until smooth.

3 Meanwhile remove the outer skins from the thawed broad beans and discard.

4 Cut the remaining asparagus into 5cm/2in lengths, trimming off any fibrous stems, and blanch in boiling water for 2 minutes.

5 Cook the tagliatelle in plenty of boiling salted water according to the instructions on the packet until *al dente*. Drain well.

6 Add the cooked asparagus and shelled beans to the sauce and reheat. Stir in the yogurt and toss into the tagliatelle. Garnish with sage leaves and serve at once.

Rigatoni with Scallop Sauce

A jewel from the sea, the scallop is what makes this sauce so special. Serve with a green salad, if liked.

INGREDIENTS

Serves 4

350g/12oz rigatoni
350g/12oz queen scallops
45ml/3 tbsp olive oil
1 garlic clove, chopped
1 onion, chopped
2 carrots, cut into matchsticks
30 ml/2 tbsp chopped fresh parsley
30ml/2 tbsp dry white wine
30ml/2 tbsp Pernod
150ml/¼ pint/⅔ cup double cream
salt and ground black pepper

1 Cook the pasta in plenty of boiling salted water according to the instructions on the packet.

2 Trim the scallops, separating the corals from the white eye part of the meat.

3 Using a sharp knife, cut the eye in half lengthways.

4 Heat the oil in a frying pan and fry the garlic, onion and carrots for 5–10 minutes until the carrots are softened.

5 Stir in the scallops, parsley, wine and Pernod and bring to the boil. Cover and simmer for about 1 minute. Using a slotted spoon, transfer the scallops and vegetables to a plate and keep them warm until required.

6 Bring the pan juices back to the boil and boil rapidly until reduced by half. Stir in the cream and heat the sauce through.

7 Return the scallops and vegetables to the pan and heat them through. Season to taste.

8 Drain the pasta thoroughly and toss with the sauce. Serve the rigatoni immediately.

Tagliatelle with Hazelnut Pesto

Hazelnuts provide an interesting alternative to pine nuts in this delicious pesto sauce.

INGREDIENTS

Serves 4

2 garlic cloves, crushed
25g/1oz/1 cup fresh basil leaves
25g/1oz/¼ cup hazelnuts
200g/7oz/scant 1 cup skimmed milk soft cheese
225g/8oz dried tagliatelle, or 450g/1lb fresh
salt and ground black pepper

1 Place the garlic, basil, hazelnuts and cheese in a blender or food processor and process to form a thick paste.

2 Cook the tagliatelle in plenty of lightly salted boiling water according to the instructions on the packet until just tender, then drain thoroughly.

3 Spoon the sauce into the hot pasta, tossing until melted. Sprinkle with ground black pepper to taste and serve hot.

Spaghetti with Tuna Sauce

A speedy midweek meal, which can also be made with other pasta shapes, for a change.

INGREDIENTS

Serves 4

225g/8oz dried spaghetti, or 450g/1lb fresh
1 garlic clove, crushed
400g/14oz can chopped tomatoes
425g/15oz can tuna fish in brine, flaked
2.5ml/½ tsp chilli sauce (optional)
4 stoned black olives, chopped
salt and ground black pepper

COOK'S TIP

If fresh tuna is available, use 450g/1lb cut into small chunks, and add after step 2. Simmer for 6–8 minutes, then add the chilli, olives and pasta.

1 Cook the spaghetti in plenty of lightly salted boiling water, according to the instructions on the packet, or until *al dente*. Drain well and keep hot until required.

2 Place the garlic and tomatoes in the saucepan and bring to the boil. Simmer, uncovered, for about 2–3 minutes.

3 Add the tuna, chilli sauce, if using, the olives and spaghetti. Heat well, add the seasoning to taste and serve hot.

Pasta with Pesto Sauce

Don't stint on the fresh basil – this is the most wonderful sauce in the world! And it tastes completely different from the ready-made pesto sold in jars.

INGREDIENTS

Serves 4

2 garlic cloves
50g/2oz/½ cup pine nuts
40g/1½oz/1 cup fresh basil leaves
150ml/¼ pint/⅔ cup olive oil
50g/2oz/4 tbsp unsalted butter, softened
60ml/4 tbsp freshly grated Parmesan cheese
450g/1lb spaghetti
salt and ground black pepper

1 Peel the garlic and process in a blender or food processor with a little salt and the pine nuts until broken up. Add the basil leaves and continue mixing to a paste.

2 Gradually add the olive oil, little by little, until the mixture is creamy and thick.

3 Beat in the butter and season with ground black pepper. Beat in the cheese. Alternatively, you can make the pesto by hand using a pestle and mortar.

4 Store the pesto sauce in a jar, with a layer of olive oil on top to exclude the air, in the fridge until needed.

5 Cook the pasta in plenty of boiling salted water according to the instructions on the packet, until *al dente*. Drain well.

6 Toss the pasta with half the pesto and serve in warm bowls, with the remaining pesto sauce spooned over the top.

Spaghetti with Feta Cheese

We think of pasta as being essentially Italian but, in fact, the Greeks have a great appetite for it too. It complements tangy, full-flavoured feta cheese beautifully in this simple but effective dish.

INGREDIENTS

Serves 2–3

115g/4oz spaghetti
1 garlic clove
30ml/2 tbsp extra virgin olive oil
8 cherry tomatoes, halved
a little freshly grated nutmeg
salt and ground black pepper
75g/3oz feta cheese, crumbled
15ml/1 tbsp chopped fresh basil
a few black olives, to serve (optional)

1 Cook the spaghetti in plenty of boiling salted water according to the instructions on the packet, then drain well.

2 In the same pan gently heat the garlic clove in the olive oil for 1–2 minutes, then add the halved cherry tomatoes.

3 Increase the heat to fry the tomatoes lightly for 1 minute, then remove the garlic and discard.

4 Toss in the spaghetti, season with the nutmeg and salt and pepper to taste, then stir in the crumbled feta cheese and basil.

5 Check the seasoning, remembering that feta can be quite salty, and serve hot topped with black olives, if desired.

SIMPLE SUPPERS

Tortelli with Pumpkin Stuffing

During autumn and winter the northern Italian markets are full of bright orange pumpkins which are used to make soups and pasta dishes. This flavoursome dish is a speciality of Mantua.

INGREDIENTS

Serves 6–8

1kg/2¼lb pumpkin (weight with shell)
75g/3oz/1½ cups amaretti biscuits, crushed
2 eggs
75g/3oz/¾ cup freshly grated Parmesan cheese
pinch of grated nutmeg
plain breadcrumbs, as required
egg pasta sheets made with 3 eggs
salt and ground black pepper

To serve

115g/4oz/½ cup butter
75g/3oz/¾ cup freshly grated Parmesan cheese

1 Preheat the oven to 190°C/375°F/Gas 5. Then cut the pumpkin into 10cm/4in pieces, leaving the skin on. Place the pumpkin pieces in a covered casserole and bake for about 45–50 minutes. When cool, cut off the skins. Purée the flesh in a food mill, blender or food processor or press through a sieve with a wooden spoon.

2 Combine the pumpkin purée with the biscuit crumbs, eggs, Parmesan and nutmeg. Season with salt and pepper. If the mixture is too wet, add about 15–30ml/1–2 tbsp breadcrumbs. Set aside until required.

3 Prepare the sheets of egg pasta. Roll out very thinly by hand or machine. Do not let the pasta dry out before filling.

4 Place tablespoonfuls of filling every 6cm/2½in along the pasta in rows 5cm/2in apart. Cover with another sheet of pasta, and press down gently. Use a fluted pastry or pasta wheel to cut between the rows to form rectangles with filling in the centre of each. Place the tortelli on a lightly floured surface, and allow to dry for at least 30 minutes, turning occasionally to dry both sides.

5 Bring a large pan of salted water to the boil. Gently heat the butter over a very low heat, taking care that it does not darken.

6 Drop the tortelli into the boiling water. Stir to prevent them from sticking. They will be cooked in 4–5 minutes. Drain and arrange in individual dishes. Spoon over the melted butter, sprinkle with grated Parmesan cheese and serve at once.

Stuffed Pasta Half-moons

These stuffed egg pasta half-moons are filled with a delicate mixture of cheeses. They make an elegant first course as well as a good supper.

INGREDIENTS

Serves 6–8

225g/8oz/1¼ cups fresh ricotta or curd cheese
225g/8oz/1¼ cups mozzarella cheese
115g/4oz/1 cup freshly grated Parmesan cheese
2 eggs
45ml/3 tbsp finely chopped fresh basil
salt and ground black pepper
egg pasta sheets made with 3 eggs

For the sauce
450g/1lb fresh tomatoes
30ml/2 tbsp olive oil
1 small onion, very finely chopped
90ml/6 tbsp cream

1 Press the ricotta or curd cheese through a sieve or strainer. Chop the mozzarella into very small cubes. Combine all three cheeses in a bowl. Beat in the eggs and basil, season and set aside.

2 Make the sauce by dropping the tomatoes into a small pan of boiling water for 1 minute. Remove, and peel using a small sharp knife to pull off the skins. Chop the tomatoes finely. Heat the oil in a medium saucepan. Add the onion and cook over a moderate heat until soft and translucent. Add the tomatoes and cook until soft, about 15 minutes. Season with salt and pepper. (The sauce may be pressed through a sieve to make it smooth.) Set aside.

3 Prepare the sheets of egg pasta. Roll out very thinly by hand or machine. Do not let the pasta dry out before filling.

4 Using a glass or pastry cutter, cut out rounds approximately 10cm/4in in diameter. Spoon one large tablespoon of the cheese filling on to one half of each pasta round and fold over.

5 Press the edges closed with a fork. Re-roll any trimmings and use to make more rounds. Allow the half-moons to dry for at least 10–15 minutes. Turn them over so they dry evenly.

6 Bring a large pan of salted water to the boil. Meanwhile, place the tomato sauce in a small saucepan and heat gently. Stir in the cream. Do not allow to boil.

7 Gently drop in the stuffed pasta, and stir carefully to prevent them from sticking. Cook for 5–7 minutes. Scoop them out of the water, drain carefully, and arrange in individual dishes. Spoon on some sauce to serve.

Baked Vegetable Lasagne

Following the principles of the classic meat sauce lasagne, other combinations of ingredients can be used most effectively. This vegetarian lasagne uses tomatoes and wild and cultivated mushrooms.

INGREDIENTS

Serves 8

egg pasta sheets made with 3 eggs
30ml/2 tbsp olive oil
1 onion, very finely chopped
500g/1¼lb tomatoes, fresh or canned, chopped
675g/1½lb cultivated or wild mushrooms, or a combination of both
75g/3oz/⅓ cup butter
2 garlic cloves, finely chopped
juice of ½ lemon
1 litre/1¾ pints/4 cups béchamel sauce
salt and ground black pepper
175g/6oz/1½ cups freshly grated Parmesan or Cheddar cheese, or a combination of both

1 Butter a large shallow baking dish, preferably rectangular or square in shape.

2 Make the egg pasta. Do not let it dry out before cutting into rectangles measuring about 11cm/4½in wide and the same length as the baking dish (this will make it easier to assemble).

3 In a small frying pan heat the oil and sauté the onion until translucent. Add the chopped tomatoes and cook for about 6–8 minutes, stirring often. Season with salt and pepper and set aside until required.

4 Wipe the mushrooms carefully with a damp cloth. Slice finely. Heat 40g/1½oz/3 tbsp of the butter in a frying pan and, when it is bubbling, add the mushrooms. Cook until the mushrooms start to exude their juices. Add the garlic and lemon juice, and season with salt and pepper. Cook until the liquids have almost all evaporated and the mushrooms are starting to brown. Set aside.

5 Preheat the oven to 200°C/400°F/Gas 6. Bring a very large pan of water to the boil. Place a large bowl of cold water near the cooker. Cover a large work surface with a tablecloth. Add salt to the rapidly boiling water. Drop in three or four of the egg pasta rectangles. Cook very briefly, about 30 seconds. Remove from the pan using a slotted spoon and then drop into the cold water for about 30 seconds. Remove and lay out to dry. Continue with the remaining pasta.

6 To assemble the lasagne, spread one large spoonful of the béchamel sauce over the base of the dish. Arrange a layer of pasta in the dish, cutting it with a sharp knife to fit. Cover with a thin layer of mushrooms, then one of béchamel sauce. Sprinkle with a little cheese.

7 Make another layer of pasta, spread with a thin layer of tomatoes, and then one of béchamel. Sprinkle with cheese. Repeat the layers in the same order, ending with a layer of pasta coated with béchamel. Do not make more than about six layers of pasta. Use the pasta trimmings to patch any gaps in the pasta. Sprinkle with more cheese and dot with butter.

8 Bake for 20 minutes. Remove from the oven and allow to stand for 5 minutes before serving.

Ravioli with Ricotta and Spinach

Home-made ravioli are fun to make and can be stuffed with different meat, cheese or vegetable fillings. This filling is easy to make and lighter than the more normal meat variety.

INGREDIENTS

Serves 4

400g/14oz fresh spinach or 175g/6oz frozen spinach
175g/6oz/¾ cup ricotta cheese
1 egg
50g/2oz/½ cup grated Parmesan cheese
pinch of grated nutmeg
egg pasta sheets made with 3 eggs
salt and ground black pepper

For the sauce
75g/3oz/⅓ cup butter
5–6 fresh sage sprigs

1 If using fresh spinach wash well in several changes of water. Place in a saucepan with only the water that is clinging to the leaves. Cover and cook until tender, about 5 minutes, then drain. Cook frozen spinach according to the instructions on the packet. When the spinach is cool, squeeze out as much moisture as possible then chop the leaves finely.

2 Combine the chopped spinach with the ricotta, egg, Parmesan and nutmeg. Mix well. Season with salt and pepper. Cover the bowl and set aside.

3 Prepare the sheets of egg pasta. Roll out very thinly by hand or machine. Do not let the pasta dry out before filling.

4 Place small teaspoonfuls of filling along the pasta in rows 5cm/2in apart. Cover with another sheet of pasta, pressing down gently to avoid forming any air pockets inside the ravioli.

5 Use a fluted pastry or pasta wheel to cut between the rows to form small squares with filling in the centre of each. If the edges do not stick well, moisten with milk or water and press together with a fork. Place the ravioli on a lightly floured surface, and allow to dry for at least 30 minutes, turning occasionally. Bring a large pan of salted water to the boil.

6 Heat the butter and sage together over a very low heat, taking care that the butter does not darken at all.

7 Drop the ravioli into the boiling water. Stir gently to prevent them from sticking. They will be cooked in very little time, about 4–5 minutes. Drain carefully and arrange in individual serving dishes. Spoon over the sauce and serve at once.

Baked Macaroni with Cheese

This delicious dish is perhaps less common in Italy than other pasta dishes, but has become a family favourite around the world.

INGREDIENTS

Serves 6

475ml/16fl oz/2 cups milk
1 bay leaf
3 mace blades or pinch of grated nutmeg
50g/2oz/4 tbsp butter
40g/1½oz/⅓ cup flour
175g/6oz/1½ cups grated Parmesan or Cheddar cheese, or a combination of both
40g/½oz/1/3 cup breadcrumbs
450g/1lb macaroni or other short hollow pasta
salt and ground black pepper

1 Make a béchamel sauce by gently heating the milk with the bay leaf and mace, if using, in a small saucepan. Do not let it boil. Melt the butter in a medium, heavy-based saucepan. Add the flour, and mix it in well with a wire whisk. Cook for 2–3 minutes, but do not let the butter burn. Strain the hot milk into the flour and butter mixture all at once, and mix smoothly with the whisk. Bring the sauce to the boil, stirring constantly, and cook for a further 4–5 minutes.

2 Season with salt and pepper, and the nutmeg if no mace has been used. Add all but 30ml/2 tbsp of the cheese, and stir over a low heat until melted. Place a layer of clear film right on the surface of the sauce to prevent a skin forming and set aside.

3 Preheat the oven to 200°C/400°F/Gas 6. Grease an ovenproof dish and sprinkle with some breadcrumbs. Cook the pasta in plenty of boiling salted water until *al dente*.

4 Drain the pasta, and combine it with the sauce. Pour it into the prepared dish. Sprinkle the top with the remaining breadcrumbs and grated cheese and bake in the centre of the oven for 20 minutes, until golden and bubbling.

Pasta with Roasted Pepper and Tomato

Add other vegetables such as French beans or courgettes or even chick-peas to make this sauce more substantial, if you like.

INGREDIENTS

Serves 4

2 red peppers
2 yellow peppers
45ml/3 tbsp olive oil
1 onion, sliced
2 garlic cloves, crushed
2.5ml/½ tsp mild chilli powder
400g/14oz can chopped tomatoes
450g/1lb dried pasta shells or spirals
salt and ground black pepper
freshly grated Parmesan cheese, to serve

1 Preheat the oven to 200°C/400°/Gas 6. Place the peppers on a baking sheet or in a roasting tin and bake for about 20 minutes or until they are beginning to char. Alternatively you could grill the peppers, turning frequently until evenly blistered.

2 Rub the skins off the peppers under cold water. Halve, seed and roughly chop the flesh.

3 Heat the oil in a medium saucepan and add the onion and garlic. Cook gently for 5 minutes until soft and golden.

4 Stir in the chilli powder, cook for 2 minutes, then add the tomatoes and peppers. Bring to the boil and simmer for 10–15 minutes until the sauce is slightly thickened and reduced. Season.

5 Cook the pasta in plenty of boiling salted water according to the instructions on the packet. Drain well and toss with the sauce. Serve piping hot with plenty of grated Parmesan cheese.

Tagliatelle with Walnut Sauce

An unusual sauce which would make this a spectacular dinner party starter or satisfying supper.

INGREDIENTS

Serves 4–6

2 thick slices wholemeal bread
300ml/½ pint/1¼ cups milk
275g/10oz/2½ cups walnut pieces
1 garlic clove, crushed
50g/2oz/½ cup freshly grated Parmesan cheese
90ml/6 tbsp olive oil, plus extra for tossing the pasta
150ml/¼ pint/⅔ cup double cream (optional)
450g/1lb tagliatelle
salt and ground black pepper
30ml/2 tbsp chopped fresh parsley, to garnish

1 Cut the crusts off the bread and soak in the milk until all of the milk is absorbed.

2 Preheat the oven to 190°C/375°F/Gas 5. Spread the walnuts on a baking sheet and toast in the oven for 5 minutes. Leave to cool.

3 Place the bread, walnuts, garlic, Parmesan cheese and olive oil in a blender or food processor and blend until smooth. Season to taste with salt and pepper. Stir in the cream, if using.

4 Cook the pasta in plenty of boiling salted water according to the instructions on the packet, drain and toss with a little olive oil. Divide the pasta equally among four or six bowls and place a dollop of sauce on each portion. Sprinkle with parsley.

Fusilli with Peppers and Onions

Peppers are characteristic of southern Italy. When grilled and peeled they have a delicious smoky flavour, and are easier to digest.

INGREDIENTS

Serves 4

450g/1lb red and yellow peppers
90ml/6 tbsp olive oil
1 large red onion, thinly sliced
2 garlic cloves, minced
400g/14oz fusilli or other short pasta
45ml/3 tbsp finely chopped fresh parsley
salt and ground black pepper
freshly grated Parmesan cheese, to serve

1 Place the peppers under a hot grill and turn occasionally until they are blackened and blistered on all sides. Remove from the heat, place in a plastic bag, seal and leave for 5 minutes.

2 Peel the peppers. Cut them into quarters, remove the stems and seeds, and slice into thin strips.

3 Heat the oil in a large frying pan. Add the onion, and cook over a moderate heat until translucent, 5–8 minutes. Stir in the garlic, and cook for a further 2 minutes.

4 Cook the pasta in plenty of boiling salted water until just *al dente*. Do not drain yet.

5 Meanwhile, add the peppers to the onion, and mix together gently. Stir in about 45ml/3 tbsp of the pasta cooking water. Season with salt and pepper. Stir in the finely chopped fresh parsley.

6 Drain the pasta. Tip it into the pan with the vegetables, and cook over a moderate heat for 3–4 minutes, stirring constantly to mix the pasta into the sauce. Serve with the grated Parmesan cheese handed round separately.

Ravioli with Cheese and Herbs

Vary the herbs according to what you have to hand.

INGREDIENTS

Serves 4–6

225g/8oz/1 cup full-fat soft cheese, softened

1 garlic clove, finely chopped

25g/1oz mixed herbs, such as thyme, basil, chives and parsley, finely chopped

1 quantity fresh pasta dough, rolled by machine into 2 x 30cm/12in strips, or divided into 4 and rolled by hand as thinly as possible

semolina, to coat

115g/4oz/½ cup butter

salt and ground black pepper

1 Mix together the soft cheese, garlic and most of the herbs. Season with salt and pepper.

2 Make the ravioli, filling them with the cheese and herb mixture. Toss the ravioli in a little semolina to coat lightly and leave to rest at room temperature for about 15 minutes.

3 Bring a large pan of salted water to the boil. Drop in the ravioli and cook for 7–9 minutes or until they are just tender to the bite. Drain well.

4 Melt the butter. Toss the ravioli in the melted butter. Sprinkle with the remaining herbs and serve immediately.

VARIATION

For Ravioli with Gorgonzola and Pine Nuts, fill the ravioli with a mixture of 115g/4oz/½ cup each full-fat soft cheese and crumbled Gorgonzola cheese; omit the garlic and herbs. Sprinkle the cooked ravioli with 25g/1oz/¼ cup toasted pine nuts instead of herbs.

Pasta with Courgette and Walnut Sauce

The vegetables are softened slowly to release their flavours.

INGREDIENTS

Serves 4

65g/2½oz/5 tbsp butter
1 large Spanish onion, halved and thinly sliced
450g/1lb courgettes, very thinly sliced
375g/12oz short pasta shapes, such as penne, ziti, rotini or fusilli
50g/2oz/½ cup walnuts, coarsely chopped
45ml/3 tbsp chopped fresh parsley
30ml/2 tbsp single cream
salt and ground black pepper
freshly grated Parmesan cheese, to serve

1 Melt the butter in a frying pan. Add the onion, cover and sweat for 5 minutes until translucent, then add the courgettes.

2 Stir well, cover again and sweat until the vegetables are very soft, stirring occasionally.

3 Meanwhile, cook the pasta in plenty of boiling salted water, according to the instructions on the packet, until *al dente*.

4 While the pasta is cooking, add the walnuts, parsley and cream to the courgette mixture and stir well. Season with salt and pepper.

5 Drain the pasta and return to the pan. Add the courgette sauce and mix together well. Serve immediately, with freshly grated Parmesan to sprinkle over.

Penne with Broccoli and Chilli

For a milder flavour, remove the seeds from the chilli.

INGREDIENTS

Serves 4

350g/12oz penne
450g/1lb small broccoli florets
30ml/2 tbsp stock
1 garlic clove, crushed
1 small red chilli, sliced, or 2.5ml/½ tsp chilli sauce
60ml/4 tbsp natural low-fat yogurt
30ml/2 tbsp toasted pine nuts or cashew nuts
salt and ground black pepper

1 Add the pasta to a large pan of lightly salted boiling water and return to the boil. Then place the broccoli in a steamer basket over the top. Cover and cook for about 8–10 minutes until both are just tender. Drain well.

2 Heat the stock and add the crushed garlic and chilli or chilli sauce. Stir over a low heat for 2–3 minutes.

3 Stir in the broccoli, pasta and yogurt. Adjust the seasoning, sprinkle with nuts and serve hot.

Spaghetti with Meatballs

No Italian menu would be complete without meatballs. Serve these with a light green salad if you like.

INGREDIENTS

Serves 4

For the meatballs

1 onion, chopped
1 garlic clove, chopped
350g/12oz/3 cups minced lamb
1 egg yolk
15ml/1 tbsp dried mixed herbs
15ml/1 tbsp olive oil
salt and ground black pepper

For the sauce

300ml/½ pint/1¼ cups passata
30ml/2 tbsp chopped fresh basil
1 garlic clove, chopped
salt and ground black pepper
350g/12oz spaghetti
fresh rosemary sprigs, to garnish
freshly grated Parmesan cheese, to serve

1 To make the meatballs, mix together the onion, garlic, lamb, egg yolk, herbs and seasoning until well blended.

2 Divide the mixture into about 20 pieces and mould into balls. Place on a baking sheet, cover with clear film and chill for at least 30 minutes.

3 Heat the oil in a large frying pan and add the meatballs. Fry for about 10 minutes, turning occasionally, until browned.

4 Add the passata, basil, garlic and seasoning to the pan and bring to the boil. Cover and simmer for 20 minutes, or until the meatballs are tender.

5 Meanwhile, cook the pasta in plenty of boiling salted water according to the instructions on the packet. Drain thoroughly and divide among four serving plates. Spoon over the meatballs and some of the sauce. Garnish each portion with a fresh rosemary sprig and serve immediately with plenty of freshly grated Parmesan cheese handed separately.

Pasta Salade Tiède

Boil a pan of pasta shapes and toss with vinaigrette dressing and some freshly prepared salad vegetables and you have the basis for a delicious warm salad.

INGREDIENTS

Serves 2

115g/4oz pasta shapes, such as shells
45ml/3 tbsp vinaigrette dressing
3 sun-dried tomatoes in oil, chopped
2 spring onions, sliced
25g/1oz watercress or rocket, chopped
¼ cucumber, halved, seeded and sliced
salt and ground black pepper
about 40g/1½oz pecorino cheese, coarsely grated, to garnish

1 Cook the pasta in plenty of boiling salted water according to the instructions on the packet. Drain and toss in the dressing.

2 Mix in the tomatoes, onions, watercress or rocket and cucumber. Season to taste.

3 Divide between two plates and sprinkle over the cheese. Serve at room temperature.

Penne with "Can-can" Sauce

The quality of canned pulses and tomatoes is so good that it is possible to transform them into a very fresh-tasting pasta sauce in minutes. Choose whatever pasta you like.

INGREDIENTS

Serves 3–4

225g/8oz penne
1 onion, sliced
1 red pepper, seeded and sliced
30ml/2 tbsp olive oil
400g/14oz chopped tomatoes
425g/15oz can chick-peas
30ml/2 tbsp dry vermouth (optional)
5ml/1 tsp dried oregano
1 large bay leaf
30ml/2 tbsp capers
salt and ground black pepper

1 Cook the pasta in plenty of boiling salted water according to the instructions on the packet, then drain. In a saucepan, gently fry the onion and pepper in the oil for about 5 minutes, stirring occasionally, until softened.

2 Add the tomatoes, chick-peas with their liquor, vermouth, if using, herbs and capers.

3 Season and bring to the boil, then simmer the mixture for about 10 minutes. Remove the bay leaf and mix in the pasta, reheat and serve hot.

Spaghetti with Tomato Sauce

Don't be put off by the idea of anchovies, they give a wonderful richness to the sauce, without adding their usual salty flavour.

INGREDIENTS

Serves 4

45ml/3 tbsp olive oil
1 onion, chopped
1 large garlic clove, chopped
400g/14oz can of chopped tomatoes with herbs
60ml/4 tbsp dry white wine
350g/12oz dried spaghetti
5–10ml/1–2 tsp dark soft brown sugar
50g/2oz can anchovy fillets in oil
115g/4oz pepperoni sausage, chopped
15ml/1 tbsp chopped fresh basil
salt and ground black pepper
sprigs of basil, to garnish

1 Heat the oil in a saucepan and fry the onion and garlic for 2 minutes to soften. Add the tomatoes and wine, bring to the boil and leave to simmer gently for 10–15 minutes. Put the pasta on to cook as directed.

2 After the sauce has been cooking 10 minutes add the soft brown sugar and the anchovy fillets, drained and chopped. Mix well and cook for about a further 5 minutes or so.

3 Drain the pasta and toss in very little oil. Add to it the pepperoni and the basil and sprinkle with seasoning. Serve topped with the tomato sauce and garnish with the sprigs of basil.

Tortellini with Cheese Sauce

Here is a very quick way of making a delicious cheese sauce without all the usual effort. But do eat it when really hot before the sauce starts to thicken. Blue cheese would work just as well, for a change.

INGREDIENTS

Serves 4

450g/1lb fresh tortellini
115g/4oz/½ cup ricotta or cream cheese
60–90ml/4-6 tbsp milk
50g/2oz/½ cup St Paulin or mozzarella cheese, grated
50g/2oz/½ cup Parmesan cheese, grated
2 garlic cloves, crushed
30ml/2 tbsp chopped, mixed fresh herbs, such as parsley, chives, basil or oregano
salt and ground black pepper

1 Cook the pasta according to the packet instructions, in boiling, salted water, stirring occasionally.

2 Meanwhile, gently melt the ricotta or cream cheese with the milk in a large pan. When blended, stir in the St Paulin or mozzarella, half the Parmesan, and the garlic and herbs.

3 Drain the cooked pasta and add to the pan of sauce. Stir well, and allow to cook gently for 1–2 minutes so the cheeses melt well. Season to taste and serve with the remaining Parmesan cheese sprinkled on top.

Spaghetti with Aubergine and Tomato

A great supper recipe – serve this aubergine and tomato dish with freshly cooked mange-touts.

INGREDIENTS

Serves 4

3 small aubergines
olive oil, for frying
450g/1lb spaghetti
1 quantity Classic Tomato Sauce (see Curly Lasagne with Classic Tomato Sauce)
225g/8oz fontina cheese, grated
salt and ground black pepper

1 Top and tail the aubergines and slice thinly. Arrange in a colander, sprinkling with plenty of salt between each layer. Leave to stand for about 30 minutes.

2 Rinse the aubergines under cold running water. Drain and pat dry on kitchen paper.

3 Heat plenty of oil in a large frying pan and fry the aubergine slices in batches for about 5 minutes, turning them once during the cooking time, until evenly browned.

4 Meanwhile, cook the pasta in plenty of boiling salted water according to the instructions on the packet, until *al dente*.

5 Stir the tomato sauce into the pan with the aubergines and bring to the boil. Cover and then simmer for 5 minutes.

6 Stir in the fontina cheese and salt and pepper. Continue stirring over a medium heat until the cheese melts.

7 Drain the pasta and stir into the sauce, tossing well to coat. Serve immediately.

Pasta Tubes with Meat and Cheese Sauce

The two sauces complement each other perfectly in this wonderfully flavoursome dish.

INGREDIENTS

Serves 4

350g/12oz rigatoni
salt and ground black pepper
fresh basil sprigs, to garnish

For the meat sauce

15ml/1 tbsp olive oil
350g/12oz/3 cups minced beef
1 onion, chopped
1 garlic clove, chopped
400g/14oz can chopped tomatoes
15ml/1 tbsp dried mixed herbs
30ml/2 tbsp tomato purée

For the cheese sauce

50g/2oz/¼ cup butter
50g/2oz/½ cup plain flour
450ml/¾ pint/1¾ cups milk
2 egg yolks
50g/2oz/½ cup freshly grated Parmesan cheese

1 To make the meat sauce, heat the oil in a large frying pan and fry the beef for 10 minutes, stirring occasionally until browned. Add the onion and cook for 5 minutes, stirring occasionally.

2 Stir in the garlic, tomatoes, herbs and tomato purée. Bring to the boil, cover, and simmer for about 30 minutes.

3 Meanwhile, to make the cheese sauce, melt the butter in a small saucepan, then stir in the flour and cook for 2 minutes, stirring constantly.

4 Remove the pan from the heat and gradually stir in the milk. Return the pan to the heat and bring to the boil, stirring occasionally, until thickened.

5 Add the egg yolks, cheese and seasoning and stir until the sauce is well blended.

6 Preheat the grill. Meanwhile, cook the pasta in plenty of boiling salted water according to the instructions on the packet. Drain thoroughly and turn into a large mixing bowl. Pour over the meat sauce and toss to coat.

7 Divide the pasta among four flameproof dishes. Spoon over the cheese sauce and place under the grill until brown. Serve immediately, garnished with fresh basil.

Linguine with Clams, Leeks and Tomatoes

Canned clams make this a speedy dish for those in a real hurry.

INGREDIENTS

Serves 4

350g/12oz linguine
25g/1oz/2 tbsp butter
2 leeks, thinly sliced
150ml/¼ pint/⅔ cup dry white wine
4 tomatoes, skinned, seeded and chopped
pinch of turmeric (optional)
250g/9oz can clams, drained
30ml/2 tbsp chopped fresh basil
60ml/4 tbsp crème fraîche
salt and ground black pepper

1 Cook the pasta in plenty of boiling salted water according to the instructions on the packet.

2 Meanwhile, melt the butter in a small saucepan and fry the sliced leeks for about 5 minutes until softened.

3 Add the wine, tomatoes and turmeric, bring to the boil and boil until reduced by half.

4 Stir in the clams, basil, crème fraîche and seasoning and heat through gently without boiling the sauce.

5 Drain the pasta thoroughly and toss in the clam and leek sauce. Serve immediately.

Macaroni with King Prawns and Ham

Cooked radicchio makes a novel addition to this sauce.

INGREDIENTS

Serves 4

350g/12oz short macaroni
45ml/3 tbsp olive oil
12 shelled raw king prawns
1 garlic clove, chopped
175g/6oz/generous 1 cup diced smoked ham
150ml/¼ pint/⅔ cup red wine
½ small radicchio lettuce, shredded
2 egg yolks, beaten
30ml/2 tbsp chopped fresh flat leaf parsley
150ml/¼ pint/⅔ cup double cream
salt and ground black pepper
shredded fresh basil, to garnish

1 Cook the pasta in plenty of boiling salted water, according to the instructions on the packet.

2 Meanwhile, heat the oil in a frying pan and cook the prawns, garlic and ham for about 5 minutes, stirring occasionally until the prawns are tender. Be careful not to overcook.

3 Add the wine and radicchio, bring to the boil and boil rapidly until the juices are reduced by about half.

4 Stir in the egg yolks, parsley and cream and bring almost to the boil, stirring constantly, then simmer until the sauce thickens slightly. Check the seasoning and adjust if necessary.

5 Drain the pasta thoroughly and toss in the sauce to coat. Serve immediately, garnished with some shredded fresh basil.

Penne with Aubergine and Mint Pesto

This splendid variation on the classic Italian pesto uses fresh mint rather than basil for a deliciously different flavour.

INGREDIENTS

Serves 4

2 large aubergines
450g/1lb penne
50g/2oz/½ cup walnut halves
salt and ground black pepper

For the pesto

25g/1oz fresh mint
15g/½oz flat leaf parsley
40g/1½oz/scant ½ cup walnuts
40g/1½oz finely grated Parmesan cheese
2 garlic cloves
90ml/6 tbsp olive oil

1 Cut the aubergines lengthways into 1cm/½in slices.

2 Cut the slices again crossways to give short strips.

3 Layer the strips in a colander with salt and leave to stand for 30 minutes over a plate to catch any juices. Rinse well in cool water and then drain thoroughly.

4 Place all the pesto ingredients, except the oil, in a blender or food processor. Blend until very smooth, then gradually add the oil in a thin stream until the mixture amalgamates. Season to taste.

5 Cook the penne in plenty of boiling salted water according to the instructions on the packet for about 8 minutes or until *al dente*. Add the aubergine and cook for a further 3 minutes.

6 Drain the pasta well and mix in the mint pesto and walnut halves. Serve immediately.

Chow Mein

One of the most well-known Chinese noodle dishes.

INGREDIENTS

Serves 4

225g/8oz Chinese egg noodles
30ml/2 tbsp oil
1 onion, chopped
1cm/½in piece fresh root ginger, chopped
2 garlic cloves, crushed
30ml/2 tbsp soy sauce
50ml/2fl oz/¼ cup dry white wine
10ml/2 tsp Chinese five-spice powder
450g/1lb/4 cups minced pork
4 spring onions, sliced
50g/2oz oyster mushrooms
75g/3oz bamboo shoots
15ml/1 tbsp sesame oil
prawn crackers, to serve

1 Cook the noodles in boiling water for 4 minutes and drain.

2 Meanwhile, heat the oil in a wok and add the onion, ginger, garlic, soy sauce and wine. Cook for 1 minute. Stir in the Chinese five-spice powder.

3 Add the minced pork and cook for 10 minutes, stirring constantly. Add the spring onions, oyster mushrooms and bamboo shoots and continue to cook for a further 5 minutes.

4 Stir in the noodles and sesame oil. Mix all the ingredients together well and serve at once with prawn crackers.

Macaroni Cheese with Mushrooms

Macaroni cheese is an all-time classic from the mid-week menu. Here it is served in a light creamy sauce with mushrooms and topped with pine nuts.

INGREDIENTS

Serves 4

450g/1lb quick-cooking elbow macaroni
45ml/3 tbsp olive oil
225g/8oz button mushrooms, sliced
2 fresh thyme sprigs
60ml/4 tbsp plain flour
1 vegetable stock cube
600ml/1 pint/2½ cups milk
2.5ml/½ tsp celery salt
5ml/1 tsp Dijon mustard
175g/6oz/1½ cups grated Cheddar cheese
25g/1oz/¼ cup freshly grated Parmesan cheese
25g/1oz/2 tbsp pine nuts
salt and ground black pepper

1 Cook the macaroni in plenty of boiling salted water according to the instructions on the packet.

2 Heat the oil in a heavy-based saucepan. Add the mushrooms and thyme, cover and cook over a gentle heat for 2–3 minutes. Stir in the flour and remove from the heat, add the stock cube and stir continuously until evenly blended. Add the milk, a little at a time, stirring after each addition. Add the celery salt, mustard and Cheddar cheese and season. Stir and simmer for 1–2 minutes until the sauce is thickened.

3 Preheat a moderate grill. Drain the macaroni; toss into the sauce. Turn into four individual dishes or one large flameproof gratin dish. Scatter with grated Parmesan cheese and pine nuts; grill until brown and bubbly.

COOK'S TIP

Closed button mushrooms are best for white cream sauces. Open varieties can darken a pale sauce to an unattractive sludgy grey.

Pasta with Roasted Vegetables

Sweet roasted vegetables form the basis of a rich sauce.

INGREDIENTS

Serves 4

- 1 large onion
- 1 aubergine
- 2 courgettes
- 2 peppers, preferably red or yellow, seeded
- 450g/1lb tomatoes, preferably plum
- 2–3 garlic cloves, coarsely chopped
- 60ml/4 tbsp olive oil
- 300ml/½ pint/1¼ cups smooth tomato sauce
- 50g/2oz black olives, stoned and halved
- 375–450g/12oz–1lb dried penne
- salt and ground black pepper
- 15g/½oz fresh basil, shredded, to garnish
- freshly grated Parmesan or pecorino cheese, to serve

1 Preheat the oven to 240°C/475°F/Gas 9. Cut the onion, aubergine, courgettes, peppers and tomatoes into 2.5–4cm/1–1½in chunks. Scoop out and discard the tomato seeds.

2 Spread out the vegetables in a large roasting tin. Sprinkle the garlic and oil over the vegetables and stir and turn to mix evenly. Season with salt and pepper.

3 Roast the vegetables for about 30 minutes or until they are soft and browned (don't worry if the edges are charred black). Stir after 15 minutes.

4 Scrape the vegetable mixture into a saucepan. Add the tomato sauce and olives.

5 Cook the pasta in plenty of boiling salted water, according to the instructions on the packet, until *al dente*.

6 Meanwhile, heat the tomato and roasted vegetable sauce. Taste and adjust the seasoning if necessary.

7 Drain the pasta and return to the pan. Add the tomato and roasted vegetable sauce and stir to mix well. Serve hot, sprinkled with the basil. If you like, serve with freshly grated Parmesan or pecorino cheese handed separately.

Spaghetti with Mussels and Saffron

In this recipe the pasta is tossed with a delicious pale yellow mussel sauce, streaked with yellow strands of saffron. Powdered saffron will do just as well, but don't use turmeric – the flavour will be too strong.

INGREDIENTS

Serves 4

900g/2lb live mussels, in the shell
150ml/¼ pint/⅔ cup dry white wine
2 shallots, finely chopped
25g/1oz/2 tbsp butter
2 garlic cloves, crushed
10ml/2 tsp cornflour
300ml/½ pint/1¼ cups double cream
pinch of saffron strands
juice of ½ lemon
1 egg yolk
450g/1lb spaghetti
salt and ground black pepper
chopped fresh parsley, to garnish

1 Scrub the mussels and rinse well. Pull off any "beards" and leave the mussels to soak in cold water for 30 minutes. Tap each mussel sharply after this time. Discard any that do not close straightaway.

2 Drain the mussels and place in a large saucepan. Add the wine and shallots, cover and cook, shaking frequently, over a high heat for 5–10 minutes until the mussels are open. Discard any that do not open.

3 Drain the mussels through a sieve, reserving the liquid. Remove most of the mussels from their shells, reserving some in the shell to use as a garnish. Boil the reserved liquid rapidly until reduced by half.

4 Melt the butter in another saucepan, add the garlic and cook until golden. Stir in the cornflour and gradually stir in the cooking liquid and the cream. Add the saffron and seasoning and simmer until slightly thickened.

5 Stir in lemon juice to taste, then the egg yolk and mussels. Keep warm, but do not boil.

6 Cook the pasta according to the instructions on the packet. Drain. Toss the mussels with the spaghetti, top with the reserved mussels and sprinkle with the parsley. Serve with crusty bread, if you like.

Prawns with Tagliatelle in Packets

A quick and impressive dish, easy to prepare in advance and cook at the last minute. When the paper packets are opened at the table, the filling smells wonderful.

INGREDIENTS

Serves 4

750g/1¾lb raw prawns in the shell
450g/1lb tagliatelle or similar pasta
150ml/¼ pint/⅔ cup fresh or ready-made pesto sauce
20ml/4 tsp olive oil
1 garlic clove, crushed
120ml/4fl oz/½ cup dry white wine
salt and ground black pepper

1 Preheat the oven to 200°C/400°F/Gas 6. Twist the heads off the prawns and discard.

2 Cook the tagliatelle in plenty of rapidly boiling salted water for 2 minutes only, then drain. Mix with half the pesto.

3 Cut four 30cm/12in squares of greaseproof paper and place 5ml/1 tsp olive oil in the centre of each. Pile equal amounts of pasta in the middle of each square.

4 Top with equal amounts of prawns and spoon over the remaining pesto mixed with the garlic. Season with pepper; sprinkle each with the wine.

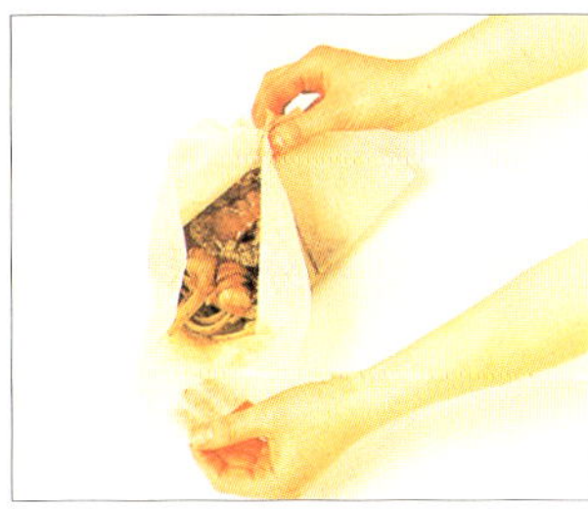

5 Brush the edges of the paper lightly with water and bring them loosely up around the filling, twisting to enclose. (The parcels should look like money bags.)

6 Place the parcels on a baking sheet. Bake in the oven for 10–15 minutes. Serve at once, allowing the diners to open their own packets at the table.

Coriander Ravioli with Pumpkin Filling

This stunning herb pasta is served with a superb creamy pumpkin and roast garlic filling.

INGREDIENTS

Serves 4–6

200g/7oz/scant 1 cup strong white flour
2 eggs
pinch of salt
45ml/3 tbsp chopped fresh coriander
coriander sprigs, to garnish

For the filling

4 garlic cloves, unpeeled
450g/1lb pumpkin, peeled and seeded
115g/4oz/½ cup ricotta cheese
4 sun-dried tomatoes in olive oil, drained and finely chopped, and 30ml/2 tbsp of the oil
ground black pepper

1 Place the flour, eggs, salt and chopped fresh coriander into a blender or food processor and pulse until combined.

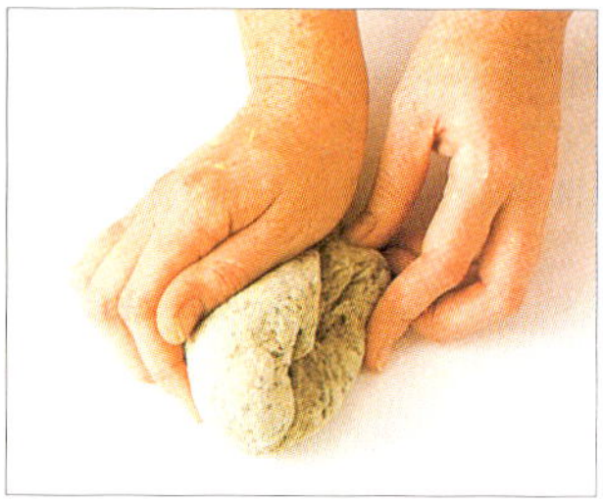

2 Place the dough on a lightly floured board and knead well for 5 minutes, until smooth. Wrap in clear film and leave to rest in the fridge for 20 minutes.

3 Preheat the oven to 200°C/400°F/Gas 6. Place the garlic cloves on a baking sheet and bake for 10 minutes until soft. Steam the pumpkin for 5–8 minutes until tender and drain well. Peel the garlic cloves and mash into the pumpkin together with the ricotta cheese and drained sun-dried tomatoes. Season with lots of ground black pepper.

4 Divide the pasta into four pieces and flatten slightly. Using a pasta machine, on its thinnest setting, roll out each piece. Leave the sheets of pasta on a clean dish towel until they are slightly dried.

5 Using a 7.5cm/3in crinkle-edged round cutter, stamp out 36 rounds of pasta.

6 Top 18 of the rounds with a teaspoonful of filling, brush the edges with water and place another round of pasta on top. Press firmly around the edges to seal. Bring a large pan of water to the boil, add the ravioli and cook for 3–4 minutes. Drain well and toss into the reserved tomato oil. Serve at once garnished with fresh coriander sprigs.

Pasta with Low-fat Pesto Sauce

Traditionally made with lashings of olive oil, this simple pesto sauce is still packed with flavour.

INGREDIENTS

Serves 4

225g/8oz dried pasta, such as spirals
50g/2oz/1 cup fresh basil leaves
25g/1oz/½ cup parsley sprigs
1 garlic clove, crushed
25g/1oz/¼ cup pine nuts
115g/4oz/½ cup curd cheese
30ml/2 tbsp freshly grated Parmesan cheese
salt and ground black pepper
fresh basil sprigs, to garnish

1 Cook the pasta in plenty of boiling salted water in a large saucepan for 8–10 minutes, or until *al dente*. Drain well.

2 Meanwhile put half the basil and half the parsley, the garlic clove, pine nuts and curd cheese into a blender or food processor fitted with a metal blade and process until smooth.

3 Add the remaining basil and parsley together with the Parmesan cheese and seasoning. Continue to process until the herbs are finely chopped.

4 Toss the pasta with the pesto and serve on warmed plates. Garnish with fresh basil sprigs.

Spinach and Hazelnut Lasagne

A vegetarian dish which is hearty enough to satisfy meat-eaters too. Use frozen spinach – you will need 450g/1lb – if you're short of time.

INGREDIENTS

Serves 4

900g/2lb fresh spinach
300ml/½ pint/1¼ cups vegetable or chicken stock
1 onion, finely chopped
1 garlic clove, crushed
75g/3oz/¾ cup hazelnuts
30ml/2 tbsp chopped fresh basil
6 lasagne sheets
400g/14oz can chopped tomatoes
200g/7oz/scant 1 cup low-fat fromage frais
flaked hazelnuts and chopped parsley, to garnish

1 Preheat the oven to 200°C/400°F/Gas 6. Wash the fresh spinach and place in a pan with just the water that clings to the leaves. Cook the spinach over a fairly high heat for 2 minutes until wilted. Drain well.

2 Heat 30ml/2 tbsp of the stock in a large pan and simmer the onion and garlic until soft. Stir in the spinach, hazelnuts and basil.

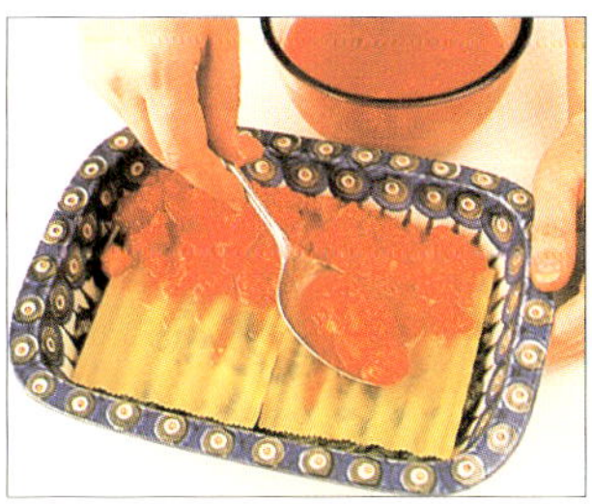

3 In a large ovenproof dish, layer the spinach, lasagne and the tomatoes. Season well between the layers. Pour over the remaining stock. Spread the low-fat fromage frais over the top.

4 Bake the lasagne for about 45 minutes, or until golden brown. Serve hot, sprinkled with lines of flaked hazelnuts and chopped parsley.

Tagliatelle with Gorgonzola Sauce

Gorgonzola is a creamy Italian blue cheese. As an alternative you could use Danish Blue or Pipo Creme.

INGREDIENTS

Serves 4

25g/1oz/2 tbsp butter, plus extra for tossing the pasta
225g/8oz Gorgonzola cheese
150ml/¼ pint/⅔ cup double or whipping cream
30ml/2 tbsp dry vermouth
5ml/1 tsp cornflour
15ml/1 tbsp chopped fresh sage
450g/1lb tagliatelle
salt and ground black pepper

1 Melt 25g/1oz/2 tbsp butter in a heavy saucepan (it needs to be thick-based to prevent the cheese from burning). Stir in 175g/6oz crumbled Gorgonzola cheese and stir over a gentle heat for about 2–3 minutes until melted.

2 Whisk in the cream, vermouth and cornflour. Add the sage; season. Cook, whisking, until the sauce boils and thickens. Set aside.

3 Boil the pasta in plenty of salted water according to the instructions on the packet. Drain well and toss with a little butter.

4 Reheat the sauce gently, whisking well. Divide the pasta among four serving bowls, top with the sauce and sprinkle over the remaining crumbled cheese. Serve immediately.

Pasta with Tomato and Cream Sauce

Here pasta is served with a deliciously rich version of an ordinary tomato sauce.

INGREDIENTS

Serves 4–6

30ml/2 tbsp olive oil
2 garlic cloves, crushed
400g/14oz can chopped tomatoes
150ml/¼ pint/⅔ cup double or whipping cream
30ml/2 tbsp chopped fresh herbs, such as basil, oregano or parsley
450g/1lb pasta, any variety
salt and ground black pepper

1 Heat the oil in a medium saucepan, add the garlic and cook for 2 minutes, until golden.

2 Stir in the tomatoes, bring to the boil and simmer uncovered for 20 minutes, stirring occasionally to prevent sticking. The sauce is ready when you can see the oil separating on top.

3 Add the cream, bring slowly to the boil again and simmer until slightly thickened. Stir in the herbs, taste and season well.

4 Cook the pasta in plenty of boiling salted water according to the instructions on the packet. Drain well and toss with the sauce. Serve piping hot, sprinkled with extra herbs, if you like.

Pasta Sauces

Ravioli with Four-cheese Sauce

This is a smooth, cheesy sauce that coats the pasta very evenly.

INGREDIENTS

Serves 4

350g/12oz ravioli
50g/2oz/¼ cup butter
50g/2oz/¼ cup plain flour
450ml/¾ pint/1¾ cups milk
50g/2oz Parmesan cheese
50g/2oz Edam cheese
50g/2oz Gruyère cheese
50g/2oz fontina cheese
salt and ground black pepper
chopped fresh flat leaf parsley, to garnish

1 Cook the pasta in plenty of boiling salted water according to the instructions on the packet.

2 Melt the butter in a saucepan, stir in the flour and cook for 2 minutes, stirring occasionally.

3 Gradually stir in the milk until completely blended.

4 Bring the milk slowly to the boil, stirring constantly until the sauce is thickened.

5 Grate the cheeses and stir them into the sauce. Stir until they are just beginning to melt. Remove from the heat and season.

6 Drain the pasta thoroughly and turn into a large serving dish. Pour over the sauce and toss to coat. Serve immediately, garnished with the chopped fresh parsley.

Spaghetti in a Cream and Bacon Sauce

This is a light and creamy sauce flavoured with bacon and lightly cooked eggs.

INGREDIENTS

Serves 4

350g/12oz spaghetti
15ml/1 tbsp olive oil
1 onion, chopped
115g/4oz rindless streaky bacon or pancetta, diced
1 garlic clove, chopped
3 eggs
300ml/½ pint/1¼ cups double cream
50g/2oz Parmesan cheese
chopped fresh basil, to garnish

1 Cook the pasta in plenty of boiling salted water according to the instructions on the packet.

2 Heat the oil in a frying pan and fry the onion and bacon or pancetta for 10 minutes, until softened. Stir in the garlic and fry for a further 2 minutes, stirring occasionally.

3 Meanwhile, beat the eggs in a bowl, then stir in the cream and seasoning. Grate the Parmesan cheese and stir into the egg and cream mixture.

4 Stir the cream mixture into the onion and bacon or pancetta and cook over a low heat for a few minutes, stirring constantly, until heated through. Season to taste.

5 Drain the pasta thoroughly and turn into a large serving dish. Pour over the sauce and toss to coat. Serve immediately, garnished with chopped fresh basil.

Pasta Twists with Cream and Cheese

Soured cream and two cheeses make a lovely rich sauce.

INGREDIENTS

Serves 4

350g/12oz pasta twists, such as spirali
25g/1oz/2 tbsp butter
1 onion, chopped
1 garlic clove, chopped
15ml/1 tbsp chopped fresh oregano
300ml/½ pint/1¼ cups soured cream
75g/3oz/¾ cup grated mozzarella cheese
75g/3oz/¾ cup grated Bel Paese cheese
5 sun-dried tomatoes in oil, drained and sliced
salt and ground black pepper

1 Cook the pasta in plenty of boiling salted water according to the instructions on the packet.

2 Melt the butter in a large frying pan and fry the onion for about 10 minutes until softened. Add the garlic and cook for 1 minute.

3 Stir in the oregano and cream and heat gently until almost boiling. Stir in the mozzarella and Bel Paese cheese and heat gently, stirring occasionally, until melted. Add the sun-dried tomatoes and season to taste.

4 Drain the pasta twists well and turn into a serving dish. Pour over the sauce and toss well to coat. Serve immediately.

Cannelloni with Cheese and Coriander

A speedy supper dish, this is best served with a simple tomato and fresh basil salad.

INGREDIENTS

Serves 4

450g/1lb cannelloni
115g/4oz full-fat garlic-and-herb cheese
30ml/2 tbsp very finely chopped fresh coriander
300ml/½ pint/1¼ cups single cream
115g/4oz/1 cup shelled peas, cooked
salt and ground black pepper

1 Cook the pasta in plenty of boiling salted water according to the instructions on the packet.

2 Melt the cheese in a small pan over a low heat until smooth.

3 Stir in the coriander, cream and salt and pepper. Bring slowly to the boil, stirring occasionally, until well blended. Stir in the peas and continue cooking until heated through.

4 Drain the pasta and turn into a large serving dish. Pour over the sauce and toss well to coat thoroughly. Serve immediately.

COOK'S TIP

If you do not like the pronounced flavour of fresh coriander, substitute another fresh herb, such as basil or flat leaf parsley.

Basic Tomato Sauce

Tomato sauce is without doubt the most popular dressing for pasta in Italy. This sauce is best made with fresh tomatoes, but works well with canned plum tomatoes.

INGREDIENTS

Serves 4

60ml/4 tbsp olive oil
1 onion, very finely chopped
1 garlic clove, finely chopped
450g/1lb tomatoes, fresh or canned, chopped with their juice
a few fresh basil leaves or parsley sprigs
salt and ground black pepper

1 Heat the oil in a medium saucepan. Add the onion, and cook over a moderate heat until it is translucent, 5–8 minutes.

2 Stir in the garlic and the tomatoes with their juice (add 45ml/3 tbsp of water if you are using fresh tomatoes). Season with salt and pepper. Add the herbs. Cook for 20–30 minutes.

3 Pass the sauce through a food mill or purée in a blender or food processor. To serve, reheat gently, correct the seasoning and pour over drained pasta.

Special Tomato Sauce

The tomatoes in this sauce are enhanced by the addition of extra vegetables. It is good served with all types of pasta.

INGREDIENTS

Serves 6

700g/1⅔lb tomatoes, fresh or canned, chopped
1 carrot, chopped
1 celery stick, chopped
1 onion, chopped
1 garlic clove, crushed
75ml/5 tbsp olive oil
a few fresh basil leaves or small pinch dried oregano
salt and ground black pepper

1 Place all the ingredients in a medium heavy saucepan, and simmer for 30 minutes.

2 Purée the sauce in a blender or food processor; alternatively press through a sieve.

COOK'S TIP

This sauce may be spooned into freezer bags and frozen until required. Allow to thaw at room temperature before reheating.

3 Return the sauce to the pan, correct the seasoning, and bring to a simmer. Cook for about 15 minutes, then pour over drained cooked pasta.

Fusilli with Mascarpone and Spinach

This creamy, green sauce tossed in lightly cooked pasta is best served with plenty of sun-dried tomato ciabatta bread.

INGREDIENTS

Serves 4

350g/12oz pasta spirals, such as fusilli
50g/2oz/¼ cup butter
1 onion, chopped
1 garlic clove, chopped
30ml/2 tbsp fresh thyme leaves
225g/8oz frozen spinach leaves, thawed
225g/8oz/1 cup mascarpone cheese
salt and ground black pepper
fresh thyme sprigs, to garnish

1 Cook the pasta in plenty of boiling salted water according to the instructions on the packet.

2 Melt the butter in a large saucepan and fry the onion for 10 minutes until softened.

3 Stir in the garlic, fresh thyme, spinach and seasoning and heat gently for about 5 minutes, stirring occasionally, until heated through.

4 Stir in the mascarpone cheese and cook gently until heated through. Do not boil.

5 Drain the pasta thoroughly and stir into the sauce. Toss until well coated. Serve immediately, garnished with fresh thyme.

COOK'S TIP

Mascarpone is a rich Italian cream cheese. If you cannot find any, use ordinary full-fat cream cheese instead.

Spaghetti with Mixed Mushrooms

This combination of mixed mushrooms and freshly chopped sweet basil tossed with spaghetti would be well complemented by a simple tomato salad.

INGREDIENTS

Serves 4

50g/2oz/¼ cup butter
1 onion, chopped
350g/12oz spaghetti
350g/12oz mixed mushrooms, such as brown, flat and button, sliced
1 garlic clove, chopped
300ml/½ pint/1¼ cups soured cream
30ml/2 tbsp chopped fresh basil
50g/2oz/½ cup freshly grated Parmesan cheese
salt and ground black pepper
torn flat leaf parsley, to garnish
freshly grated Parmesan cheese, to serve

1 Melt the butter in a large frying pan and fry the chopped onion for 10 minutes until softened.

2 Cook the pasta in plenty of boiling salted water according to the instructions on the packet.

3 Stir the mushrooms and garlic into the onion mixture and fry for 10 minutes until softened.

4 Add the soured cream, basil, grated Parmesan cheese and salt and pepper to taste. Cover and heat through.

5 Drain the pasta thoroughly and toss with the sauce. Serve immediately, garnished with torn flat leaf parsley, with plenty of grated Parmesan cheese.

Curly Lasagne with Classic Tomato Sauce

A classic sauce that is simply delicious just served by itself.

INGREDIENTS

Serves 4

30ml/2 tbsp olive oil
1 onion, chopped
30ml/2 tbsp tomato purée
5ml/1 tsp paprika
2 × 400g/14oz cans chopped tomatoes, drained
pinch of dried oregano
300ml/½ pint/1¼ cups dry red wine
large pinch of caster sugar
350g/12oz curly lasagne
salt and ground black pepper
Parmesan cheese shavings, to serve
chopped fresh flat leaf parsley, to garnish

1 Heat the oil in a large frying pan and fry the onion for 10 minutes, stirring occasionally, until softened. Add the tomato purée and paprika and cook for a further 3 minutes.

2 Add the tomatoes, oregano, wine and sugar and season to taste, then bring to the boil.

3 Simmer for 20 minutes until the sauce has reduced and thickened, stirring occasionally.

4 Meanwhile, cook the pasta in plenty of boiling salted water according to the instructions on the packet. Drain thoroughly and turn into a large serving dish. Pour over the sauce and toss to coat. Serve sprinkled with Parmesan cheese shavings and the chopped fresh flat leaf parsley.

COOK'S TIP

If you cannot find curly lasagne use plain lasagne snipped in half lengthways.

Pasta Spirals with Pesto Sauce

A light, fragrant sauce like this dish gives a temptingly different taste.

INGREDIENTS

Serves 4

- 350g/12oz pasta spirals (fusilli)
- 50g/2oz fresh basil leaves, without the stalks
- 2 garlic cloves, chopped
- 30ml/2 tbsp pine nuts
- salt and freshly ground black pepper
- 150ml/¼ pint/⅔ cup olive oil
- 50g/2oz/⅓ cup Parmesan cheese, freshly grated, plus extra to garnish
- fresh basil sprigs, to garnish

COOK'S TIP

Fresh basil is widely available from most greengrocers and supermarkets, either in growing pots or packets. If you buy a plant, remove the flowers as they appear so the plant grows more leaves.

Pesto is best kept in a screw-topped jar in the fridge for up to two days. If you want to keep it a few days longer, cover the top with a thin layer of olive oil. This can be stirred into the sauce when you are ready to add it to hot pasta.

1 Cook the pasta following the instructions on the packet until *al dente*.

2 To make the pesto sauce, place the basil leaves, garlic, pine nuts, seasoning and olive oil in a food processor or blender. Blend until very creamy.

3 Transfer the mixture to a bowl and stir in the freshly grated Parmesan cheese.

4 Drain the pasta thoroughly and turn it into a large bowl. Pour the sauce over and toss to coat. Divide among serving plates and serve, sprinkled with the extra Parmesan cheese and garnished with fresh basil sprigs.

Pasta Twists with Classic Meat Sauce

This is a rich meat sauce which is ideal to serve with all types of pasta. The sauce definitely improves if kept overnight in the fridge. This allows the flavours time to mature.

INGREDIENTS

Serves 4

- 450g/1lb/4 cups minced beef
- 115g/4oz smoked streaky beacon, rinded and chopped
- 1 onion, chopped
- 2 celery sticks, chopped
- 15ml/1 tbsp plain flour
- 150ml/¼ pint/⅔ cup chicken stock or water
- 45ml/3 tbsp tomato purée
- 1 garlic clove, chopped
- 45ml/3 tbsp chopped fresh mixed herbs, such as oregano, parsley, marjoram and chives or 15ml/1 tbsp dried mixed herbs
- 15ml/1 tbsp redcurrant jelly
- 350g/12oz pasta twists, such as spirali
- salt and ground black pepper
- chopped oregano, to garnish

1 Heat a large saucepan and fry the beef and bacon for about 10 minutes, stirring occasionally until browned.

2 Add the chopped onion and celery and cook for 2 minutes, stirring occasionally.

COOK'S TIP

The redcurrant jelly helps to draw out the flavour of the tomato purée. You can use a sweet mint jelly or chutney instead, if you like

3 Stir in the flour and cook for 2 minutes, stirring constantly.

4 Pour in the stock or water and bring to the boil.

5 Stir in the tomato purée, garlic, herbs, redcurrant jelly and seasoning. Bring to the boil, cover and simmer for about 30 minutes.

6 Cook the pasta in plenty of boiling salted water according to the instructions on the packet. Drain thoroughly and turn into a large serving dish. Pour over the sauce and toss to coat. Serve the pasta immediately, garnished with chopped fresh oregano.

Macaroni with Hazelnut and Coriander Sauce

This is a variation on pesto sauce, giving a smooth, herby flavour of coriander.

INGREDIENTS

Serves 4

350g/12oz macaroni
50g/2oz/⅓ cup hazelnuts
2 garlic cloves
1 bunch fresh coriander
1 tsp salt
90ml/6 tbsp olive oil
fresh coriander sprigs, to garnish

1 Cook the pasta following the instructions on the packet, until *al dente*.

2 Meanwhile, finely chop the hazelnuts.

COOK'S TIP

To remove the skins from the hazelnuts, place them in a 180°C/350°F/Gas 4 oven for 20 minutes, then rub off the skins with a clean dish towel.

3 Place the nuts and remaining ingredients, except 1 tbsp of the oil, in a food processor, or use a pestle and mortar and grind together to create the sauce.

4 Heat the remaining oil in a saucepan and add the sauce. Fry very gently for about 1 minute until heated through.

5 Drain the pasta thoroughly and stir it into the sauce. Toss well to coat. Serve immediately, garnished with fresh coriander.

Spaghetti with Bacon and Tomato Sauce

This substantial sauce is a meal in itself, so serve it up as a warming winter supper.

INGREDIENTS

Serves 4

15ml/1 tbsp olive oil
225g/8oz smoked streaky bacon, rinded and roughly chopped
250g/9oz spaghetti
5ml/1 tsp chilli powder
1 quantity Classic Tomato Sauce (see Curly Lasagne with Classic Tomato Sauce)
salt and ground black pepper
roughly chopped fresh flat leaf parsley, to garnish

1 Heat the oil in large frying pan and fry the bacon for about 10 minutes, stirring occasionally until crisp and golden.

2 Cook the pasta following the instructions on the packet, until *al dente*.

3 Add the chilli powder to the bacon and cook for 2 minutes. Stir in the tomato sauce and bring to the boil. Cover and simmer for 10 minutes. Season with salt and pepper to taste.

4 Drain the pasta thoroughly and toss it together with the sauce. Serve garnished with the roughly chopped fresh parsley.

Tagliattelle with Pea and Ham Sauce

A colourful sauce, this is ideal served with crusty Italian or French bread.

INGREDIENTS

Serves 4

350g/12oz tagliatelle
225g/8oz/1½ cups shelled peas
300ml/½ pint/1¼ cups single cream
50g/2oz/⅓ cup freshly grated fontina cheese
75g/3oz Parma ham, sliced into strips
salt and ground black pepper

1 Cook the pasta following the instructions on the packet until *al dente*.

2 Plunge the peas into a pan of boiling salted water and cook for about 7 minutes or until tender. Drain and set aside.

3 Place the cream and half the fontina cheese in a small saucepan and heat gently, stirring constantly until heated through.

4 Drain the pasta thoroughly and turn it into a large serving bowl. Toss together the pasta, ham and peas and pour on the sauce. Add the remaining cheese and season with salt and pepper to taste.

Index

A
Artichoke pasta salad 112
Asparagus:
pasta, asparagus and potato salad 116
tagliatelle with Parma ham and asparagus 96
tagliatelle with peas, asparagus and beans 196
tagliolini with asparagus 80
warm pasta salad with ham and egg 119
Aubergine:
aubergine lasagne 132
pasta tossed with grilled vegetables 105
pasta with caponata 155
pasta with roasted vegetables 229
penne with aubergine and mint pesto 226
spaghetti with aubergine and tomato 222
Autumn glory 154
Avocados:
avocado, tomato and mozzarella salad 120
Greek pasta with avocado sauce 188
mixed rice noodles 61
tagliatelle with haddock and avocado 49

B
Bacon:
bacon and tomato sauce 252
pasta carbonara 136
pasta with tomato and smoky bacon 147
spaghetti alla carbonara 150, 241
spaghetti with bacon and onion 102
spaghetti with eggs and bacon 171
Baked lasagne with meat sauce 162
Baked macaroni with cheese 209
Baked seafood spaghetti 52
Baked tortellini with three cheeses 157
Baked vegetable lasagne 206
Beans:
borlotti beans with mushrooms 169
butter bean and pesto pasta 125
Italian bean and pasta soup 32
pasta, bean and vegetable soup 22
tagliatelle with peas, asparagus and beans 196
see also Minestrone
Béchamel sauce 94, 161, 162
Beef:
beef strips with orange and ginger 75
cannelloni stuffed with meat 142
cheesy pasta bolognese 144
classic meat sauce 250
pasta timbales 149
pasta tubes with meat and cheese sauce 223
spicy beef 81
twin cities meatballs 78
see also Bolognese sauces
Beetroot tagliatelle 9
Black pasta with scallops 59
Bolognese sauces:
Bolognese meat sauce 135
cheesy pasta Bolognese 144
lentil Bolognese 94
pasta with Bolognese sauce 151
peasant Bolognese 79
Broccoli:
broccoli and ricotta cannelloni 156
orecchiette with broccoli 170
penne with broccoli and chilli 216

C
Campanelle 9, 180
campanelle with yellow pepper sauce 180
"Can-can" sauce 218
Cannelloni 9, 158
broccoli and ricotta cannelloni 156
cannelloni al forno 98
cannelloni stuffed with meat 142
cannelloni with cheese and coriander 242
smoked trout cannelloni 50
Capellini with rocket and mange-touts 87

Capers 10
Caponata, pasta with 155
Cappelletti 8
Caramellone 8
Carbonara sauce 10
mushroom and chilli carbonara 176
pasta carbonara 136
spaghetti alla carbonara 150, 241
Cauliflower:
Parmesan and cauliflower soup 31
short pasta with cauliflower 102
Caviar, spaghettini with vodka and 58
Cheese:
baked macaroni cheese 136
baked macaroni with cheese 209
baked tortellini with three cheeses 157
broccoli and ricotta cannelloni 156
cannelloni with cheese and coriander 242
cheesy pasta bolognese 144
cream and cheese sauce 242
creamy Parmesan and cauliflower soup 31
four cheese sauce 240
fusilli with mascarpone and spinach 246
leek and chèvre lasagne 164
macaroni and blue cheese 165
macaroni cheese with mushrooms 228
macaroni soufflé 133
pasta spirals with lentils and cheese 159
pasta tubes with meat and cheese sauce 223
pasta with prawns and feta cheese 62
ravioli with cheese and herbs 214
ravioli with ricotta and spinach 208
Roquefort and walnut pasta salad 117
spaghetti with feta cheese 201
spinach and ricotta conchiglie 106
stuffed pasta half-moons 205
tagliatelle with Gorgonzola sauce 236
tortellini with cheese sauce 220
tortellini with cream, butter and cheese 187
Chicken:
cannelloni al forno 98
chicken and pasta salad 129
chicken lasagne 141
chicken pasta salad 114
chicken vermicelli soup with egg shreds 30
pasta spirals with chicken and tomato 160
penne with chicken and ham sauce 195
stir-fried sweet and sour chicken 82
tagliatelle with chicken and herb sauce 100
Thai chicken soup 24, 30
Thai fried noodles 145
Chilli:
bacon, chilli and tomato sauce 252
mushroom and chilli carbonara 176
penne with broccoli and chilli 216
Chinese-style vegetable and noodle soup 29
Chorizo sausage:
pasta spirals with pepperoni and tomato 83
pasta twists with mushroom and chorizo 194
peasant Bolognese 79
penne with sausage and Parmesan sauce 101
Chow mein 227
Chunky pasta soup 23
Clams:
linguine with clam and tomato sauce 71
linguine with clam, leek and tomato 224
spaghetti with clams 41
spaghetti with seafood sauce 68
spaghetti with tomato and clam sauce 40
Classic minestrone 25
Conchigliette rigate 9
Courgettes:
courgette soup with small pasta shells 33
pasta tossed with grilled vegetables 105
pasta with caponata 155
pasta with courgette and walnut sauce 215
pasta with roasted vegetables 229
Crab:
consommé with agnolotti 27
seafood pasta shells with spinach sauce 44

E
Egg pasta 14
cooking 17
green 16
making by hand 14-15
making by machine 16
Eggs:
spaghetti alla carbonara 150, 241
spaghetti with eggs and bacon 171
Equipment 12-13

F
Farfalle (pasta bows) 9
farfalle with prawns and peas 84
pasta bows with fennel and walnut 104
pasta bows with smoked salmon and dill 46
short pasta with spring vegetables 84
Fettuccia riccia 9
Fettuccine 15
fettuccine all'Alfredo 190
fettuccine with ham and cream 76
pasta with Bolognese sauce 151
pasta with scallops and tomato sauce 51
Fish:
Mediterranean salad with basil 126
pasta bows with smoked salmon and dill 46
pasta tubes with tuna and olive sauce 56
pasta with fresh sardine sauce 69
pasta with tuna, capers and anchovies 42
penne with tuna and mozzarella 58
Provençal fish soup with pasta 35
salmon pasta with parsley sauce 38
smoked trout cannelloni 50
smoked trout pasta salad 113
spaghetti with hot-and-sour fish 57
spaghetti with tuna sauce 198
tagliatelle with haddock and avocado 49
tagliatelle with smoked salmon 64, 76
tuna lasagne 55
tuna pasta salad 114
Fried Singapore noodles 60
Fusilli (pasta spirals):
curly spaghetti with walnut and cream 97
fusilli with mascarpone and spinach 246
fusilli with peppers and onions 212
fusilli with turkey 139
fusilli with vegetable and prawn sauce 54
mixed summer pasta 65

pasta spirals with chicken and tomato 160
pasta spirals with lentils and cheese 159
pasta spirals with pepperoni and tomato 83
pasta spirals with pesto sauce 234, 249
pasta with courgette and walnut sauce 215
short pasta with spring vegetables 84

G
Garganelle 9, 18
pasta with prawns and feta cheese 62
pasta with tuna, capers and anchovies 42
Garlic 10
Golden-topped pasta 90
Greek pasta bake 134
Greek pasta with avocado sauce 188

H
Haddock:
tagliatelle with haddock and avocado 49
Ham (*see also* Prosciutto):
macaroni with king prawns and ham 224
pasta carbonara 136
pea and ham sauce 252
pea and ham soup 26
penne with chicken and ham sauce 195
tagliatelle with Parma ham and asparagus 96
warm pasta salad with ham and egg 119
Hazelnuts:
hazelnut and coriander sauce 251
hazelnut pesto 198
spinach and hazelnut lasagne 235

I
Italian bean and pasta soup 32

K
Kidneys:
pasta with devilled kidneys 90

L
Lamb:
Greek pasta bake 134
spaghetti with meatballs 217
Lasagne 8, 9, 15
aubergine lasagne 132
baked lasagne with meat sauce 162
baked vegetable lasagne 206
chicken lasagne 141
curly lasagne with classic tomato sauce 248
lasagne al forno 161
lasagne rolls 94
leek and chèvre lasagne 164
spinach and hazelnut lasagne 235
tuna lasagne 55
Leeks:
leek and chèvre lasagne 164
see also Mushroom and chilli carbonara
Lentils:
lentil Bolognese 94
pasta spirals with lentils and cheese 159
Linguine:
linguine with clam and tomato sauce 71
linguine with clams, leeks and tomatoes 224
linguine with pesto sauce 168
linguine with sweet pepper and cream 192
pasta with scallops and tomato sauce 51

M
Macaroni 8, 18
baked macaroni with cheese 209
macaroni and blue cheese 165
macaroni cheese with mushrooms 228
macaroni soufflé 133
macaroni with hazelnut and coriander sauce 251
macaroni with king prawns and ham 224
pasta bake 136
pasta timbales 149
turkey pastitsio 138
Magnificent marrow 99
Mascarpone and spinach, fusilli with 246
Meatballs 217
twin cities meatballs 78
Mediterranean salad with basil 126
Minestrone 34
classic minestrone 25
minestrone with pesto toasts 124

Mixed rice noodles 61
Mixed summer pasta 65
Mushrooms:
baked vegetable lasagne 206
pappardelle, beans and mushrooms 169
macaroni cheese with mushrooms 228
mushroom and chilli carbonara 176
mushroom paste 10
oriental vegetable noodles 92
pasta twists with mushroom and chorizo 194
spaghetti with mixed mushrooms 247
spaghetti with olives and mushrooms 181
Mussels:
baked seafood spaghetti 52
seafood spaghetti 193
spaghetti with mixed shellfish sauce 47
spaghetti with mussels 66
spaghetti with mussels and saffron 230
tagliatelle with saffron mussels 39

N
Napoletana, pasta 175
Noodles 11
beef strips with orange and ginger 75
chow mein 227
fried Singapore noodles 60
mixed rice noodles 61
noodles with prawns in lemon sauce 43
noodles with Italian mushrooms 140
oriental vegetable noodles 92
sesame noodle salad with hot peanuts 122
spicy beef 81
stir-fried sweet and sour chicken 82
Thai chicken soup 30
Thai fried noodles 145
twin cities meatballs 78

O
Olive paste 10
Olives:
pasta salad with olives 111
pasta tubes with tuna and olive sauce 56
spaghetti with olives and capers 70
spaghetti with olives and mushrooms 181
Orecchiette 9
Orecchiette with broccoli 170
Oriental vegetable noodles 92
Orzo 8

P
Paglia e fieno 174
Pappardelle 9, 15, 18
pappardelle, beans and mushrooms 169
pasta tossed with grilled vegetables 105
saffron pappardelle 58
Parsley pesto, pasta rapido with 89
Passata 10
Pasta 8-9, 11, 14-17
see Farfalle; Fettuccine; Fusilli; Linguine; Garganelle; Macaroni; Pappardelle; Pasta shells; Pasta twists; Penne; Ravioli; Rigatoni; Spaghetti; Tagliatelle
Pasta shells 9
pasta and beetroot salad 118
pasta shells with tomatoes and rocket 189
Pasta timbales 149
Pasta twists:
with classic meat sauce 250
with cream and cheese 242
with mushroom and chorizo 194
Pastes 10
Pastitsio 134
turkey pastitsio 138
Peas:
paglia e fieno 174
pea and ham sauce 252
pea and ham soup 26
tagliatelle with peas, asparagus and beans 196
Peasant Bolognese 79
Penne:
with aubergine and mint pesto 226
with broccoli and chilli 216
with "can-can" sauce 218
with chicken and ham sauce 195
with courgette and walnut sauce 215
with prawns and feta cheese 62
with roasted vegetables 229
with sausage and Parmesan sauce 101
with spring vegetables 84, 182
with tuna, capers and anchovies 42
see also Orecchiette with broccoli
Peppers:
fusilli with peppers and onions 212
linguine with sweet pepper and cream 192
pasta with roasted pepper and tomato 210
Pesto 10, 200, 249
butter bean and pesto pasta 125
hazelnut pesto 198
minestrone with pesto toasts 124
mint pesto 226
simple low-fat pesto 234
Pipe rigate 9
Pork:
chow mein 227
Thai fried noodles 145
twin cities meatballs 78
Prawns:
baked seafood spaghetti 52
farfalle with prawns and peas 84
fried Singapore noodles 60
fusilli with vegetable and prawn sauce 54
macaroni with king prawns and ham 224
mixed summer pasta 65
noodles with prawns in lemon sauce 43
pasta, melon and prawn salad 128
pasta with prawns and feta cheese 62
prawns with tagliatelle in packets 231
seafood spaghetti 193
seafood pasta shells with spinach sauce 44
spaghetti with mixed shellfish sauce 47
spaghetti with seafood sauce 68
Prosciutto:
fettuccine with ham and cream 76
tagliatelle with prosciutto and Parmesan 86
Provençal fish soup with pasta 35
Pumpkin:
autumn glory 154
coriander ravioli with pumpkin filling 232
tortelli with pumpkin stuffing 204
Puntalette 8

R
Ravioli 8
coriander ravioli with pumpkin filling 232
home-made 19, 152
ravioli with cheese and herbs 214
ravioli with four-cheese sauce 240
ravioli with ricotta and spinach 208
Rigatoni (pasta tubes) 9
pasta tubes with meat and cheese sauce 223

pasta tubes with tuna and olive sauce 56
pasta with prawns and feta cheese 62
pasta with roasted vegetables 229
pasta with tuna, capers and anchovies 42
rigatoni with garlic crumbs 172
rigatoni with scallop sauce 197
rigatoni with spicy sausage 146
Roquefort and walnut pasta salad 117
Rotolo di pasta 148

S
Salads:
artichoke pasta salad 112
avocado, tomato and mozzarella salad 120
chicken and pasta salad 129
chicken pasta salad 114
Mediterranean salad with basil 126
pasta and beetroot salad 118
pasta, asparagus and potato salad 116
pasta, melon and prawn salad 128
pasta salade tiède 218
pasta salad with olives 111
Roquefort and walnut pasta salad 117
sesame noodle salad with hot peanuts 122
smoked trout pasta salad 113
tuna pasta salad 114
warm pasta salad 119
wholemeal pasta salad 110
Salmon:
salmon pasta with parsley sauce 38
see also Smoked salmon
Salsa sauce, "hit-the-pan" 177
Sardines:
pasta with fresh sardine sauce 69
Sausages (*see also* chorizo sausage):
rigatoni with spicy sausage 146
Scallops:
black pasta with scallops 59
pasta with scallops and tomato sauce 51
rigatoni with scallop sauce 197
Seafood pasta shells with spinach sauce 44
Seafood spaghetti 193
Sesame noodle salad with hot peanuts 122
Shellfish *see* Clams; Mussels; Prawns; Scallops
Short pasta with spring vegetables 84
Smoked salmon:
pasta bows with smoked salmon and dill 46
tagliatelle with smoked salmon 64, 76
Smoked trout *see* Trout, smoked
Soufflé, macaroni 133
Soups:
chicken vermicelli soup with egg shreds 30
Chinese-style vegetable and noodle soup 29
chunky pasta soup 23
consommé with agnolotti 27
courgette soup with small pasta shells 33
Italian bean and pasta soup 32
minestrone 34
classic minestrone 25
with pesto toasts 124
Parmesan and cauliflower soup 31
pasta, bean and vegetable soup 22
pea and ham soup 26
Provençal fish soup with pasta 35
red onion and beetroot soup 28
Thai chicken soup 24, 30
Spaghetti 9
baked seafood spaghetti 52
mushroom and chilli carbonara 176
peasant Bolognese 79
piquant chicken with spaghetti 123
seafood spaghetti 193
spaghetti alla carbonara 150
spaghetti in a cream and bacon sauce 241
spaghetti olio e aglio 184
spaghetti with aubergine and tomato 222
spaghetti with bacon and onion 102
spaghetti with bacon and tomato sauce 252
spaghetti with Bolognese sauce 151
spaghetti with clams 41
spaghetti with eggs and bacon 171
spaghetti with feta cheese 201
spaghetti with garlic and oil 178

spaghetti with herb sauce 74
spaghetti with hot-and-sour fish 57
spaghetti with meatballs 217
spaghetti with mixed mushrooms 247
spaghetti with mixed shellfish sauce 47
spaghetti with mussels 66
spaghetti with mussels and saffron 230
spaghetti with olives and capers 70
spaghetti with olives and mushrooms 181
spaghetti with pesto sauce 200, 234
spaghetti with seafood sauce 68
spaghetti with tomato and clam sauce 40
spaghetti with tomato sauce 186, 220
spaghetti with tuna sauce 198
spaghetti with walnut sauce 178
Spicy beef 81
Spinach:
fusilli with mascarpone and spinach 246
mixed rice noodles 61
pasta with spinach and anchovy sauce 48
ravioli with ricotta and spinach 208
rotolo di pasta 148
spinach and hazelnut lasagne 235
spinach and ricotta conchiglie 106
spinach, ricotta and Parmesan filling (for stuffed pasta) 19
tagliatelle with spinach and garlic cheese 183
Spinach lasagne 9
Spinach pasta 16, 18
Squid:
spaghetti with mixed shellfish sauce 47
Stir-fried sweet and sour chicken 82
Stir-fried vegetables with pasta 93
Stuffed pasta half-moons 205

T
Tagliarini:
oriental vegetable noodles 92
Tagliatelle 8, 9, 15, 18
paglia e fieno 174
pasta carbonara 136
pasta with caponata 155
prawns with tagliatelle in packets 231
tagliatelle with Bolognese sauce 151
tagliatelle with caponata 155
tagliatelle with chicken and herb sauce 100
tagliatelle with Gorgonzola sauce 236
tagliatelle with haddock and avocado 49
tagliatelle with hazelnut pesto 198
tagliatelle with "hit-the-pan" salsa 177
tagliatelle with Parma ham and asparagus 96
tagliatelle with pea and ham sauce 252
tagliatelle with peas, asparagus and beans 196
tagliatelle with prosciutto and Parmesan 86
tagliatelle with saffron mussels 39
tagliatelle with smoked salmon 64, 76
tagliatelle with spinach and garlic cheese 183
tagliatelle with sun-dried tomatoes 88
tagliatelle with walnut sauce 211
Tagliolini 15
tagliolini with asparagus 80
Thai chicken soup 24, 30
Thai fried noodles 145
Tomatoes (canned, chopped, fresh) 10
avocado, tomato and mozzarella salad 120
baked vegetable lasagne 206
basic tomato sauce 244
curly lasagne with classic tomato sauce 248
linguine with clam and tomato sauce 71
noodles with tomato and mushroom 140
pasta napoletana 175
pasta shells with tomatoes and rocket 189
pasta with tomato and cream sauce 237
pasta with tomato and smoky bacon 147
ready-made pasta sauce 10
spaghetti with fresh tomato sauce 186
spaghetti with tomato sauce 220
spaghetti with tomato and clam sauce 40
special tomato sauce 244
tagliatelle with sun-dried tomatoes 88
tomato and cream sauce 237
Tomato pasta sauce 10
Tomato purée 10, 159
Tortelli with pumpkin stuffing 204
Tortellini 19
baked tortellini with three cheeses 157
tortellini with cheese sauce 220
tortellini with cream, butter and cheese 187
Trout, smoked:
smoked trout cannelloni 50
smoked trout pasta salad 113
Tuna:
Mediterranean salad with basil 126
pasta tubes with tuna and olive sauce 56
pasta with tuna, capers and anchovies 42
saffron pappardelle 58
spaghetti with tuna sauce 198
tuna lasagne 55
tuna pasta salad 114
Turkey:
fusilli with turkey 139
turkey pastitsio 138
Twin cities meatballs 78

V
Vegetables (*see also specific vegetables*):
Chinese-style vegetable and noodle soup 29
chunky pasta soup 23
fusilli with vegetable and prawn sauce 54
golden-topped pasta 90
minestrone *see* Minestrone
mixed summer pasta 65
pasta with caponata 155
pasta with roasted vegetables 229
pasta with spring vegetables 182
penne with "can-can" sauce 218
sesame noodle salad with hot peanuts 122
short pasta with spring vegetables 84
stir-fried vegetables with pasta 93
see also Salads
Vermicelli 8, 11
chicken vermicelli soup with egg shreds 30

W
Walnuts:
courgette and walnut sauce 215
curly spaghetti with walnut and cream 97
pasta bows with fennel and walnut 104
Roquefort and walnut pasta salad 117
walnut sauce 211
Warm pasta salad 119
Wholemeal pasta:
pasta, asparagus and potato salad 116
wholemeal pasta salad 110
Won ton skins 11

NOTES

Notes

Notes

Notes

Notes

Notes

Notes

Notes